Are You Sure You're Right?

Evangelicals and the Church of God

By Jerry A. Hickson

Warner Press

a subsidiary of Church of God Ministries, Inc.
ANDERSON, INDIANA

Coordinator of Communications and Publishing
Church of God Ministries, Inc.
PO Box 2420
Anderson, IN 46018-2420
800-848-2464
www.chog.org

To purchase additional copies of this book, to inquire about distribution and for all other sales-related matters, please contact:

Warner Press, Inc.
PO Box 2499
Anderson, IN 46018-9988
877-346-3974
www.warnerpress.com

Cover design by Carolyn Kuchar
Text design by Joseph D. Allison
Edited by Joseph D. Allison and Stephen R. Lewis

ISBN-13: 978-1-59317-138-4
ISBN-10: 1-59317-138-2

Printed in the United States of America.
06 07 08 09 10 /EP/ 10 9 8 7 6 5 4 3 2 1

Dedication

To Gilbert W. Stafford and James Earl Massey,
two of the brightest beacons that have illuminated my path

Contents

Publishers' Preface

IT IS A PRIVILEGE to publish Jerry A. Hickson's first book, *Are You Sure You Are Right?* Jerry has an unwavering commitment to Jesus Christ and the ministry of the Church of God, and this book is an important contribution to that ministry.

We are distributing several books by new voices within the movement as part of celebrating the 125th anniversary of the Church of God movement in 2006–2007. They call us to think with open hearts about what the Lord would have us do in the future. Dr. Hickson is one of these new voices.

Our role with this book is somewhat different from what we usually do as a church publishing house. The author's purpose is to challenge current beliefs and practices of the Church of God, so it's inevitable that readers will disagree with him. Even our editorial staff has reservations at several points.

For example, we believe that Jerry's criticism of predeterminism is sound; however, we believe it applies only to a small segment of the Calvinist community, whom we would call hyper-Calvinists. His critique of inerrancy is also sound, but we believe there are far more serious problems with evangelicalism's handling of the written Word. His description of the early Church of God stance on militarism is factual as far as it goes; however, we believe our history on this issue is much more complex than the discussion implies.

We could tick off other points at which we disagree or believe his statements should be qualified. But our purpose here is not to analyze Dr. Hickson's argument; these are simply examples of the critical discussions that we hope his book will inspire.

Dr. Hickson is a faithful servant of Christ and an emerging leader in the Church of God. He writes persuasively while being faithful to his own convictions, to the facts of church history, and to the full counsel of Holy Scripture. Therefore, we present this book to the church in spite of its disputable points—in large measure, because of them. May it stimulate personal introspection, serious contemplation of God's Word, and constructive dialogue within the Church of God movement as we reappraise our identity and our mission in the world.

The Publishers
Anderson, Indiana

Acknowledgements

HOW DOES one acknowledge those who have contributed to a book that is the product of a lifetime of spiritual formation? Since this book is a response to the variety of influences I have observed since childhood, the list could be long. I ask forgiveness of all I fail to mention.

My wife has been my biggest fan and faithful supporter for over twenty-five years. Elizabeth also was the product of the Church of God heritage and a family active in their local church. During our first year of marriage, my wife was employed with me in directing youth camps for the Church of God in northern Indiana. For most of the next twenty years, Elizabeth was a stay-at-home mom and a pastor's wife in settings that sometimes had unbearably high expectations of a pastor's wife. We left that world to take on the challenge of planting a church with almost no resources. After five years of fruitless effort, we moved again to enter the world of academia. At all times, Elizabeth has believed in me and been willing to accept whatever seemed to be God's calling.

Dr. Bryan Williams, chair of the department of Religion and Christian Ministries at Warner Pacific College, is singularly responsible for the impetus of this book. For years, Dr. Williams has prompted me to give attention to the development of my scholarship, over and above my teaching. During a year-end review, Dr. Williams was lavish in his assessment of my professorial work and again prodded me to engage in scholarly writing. His language this time included the suggestion that I "speak prophetically to the Church of God." Those words burned into my mind that night as I tried to go to bed. After tossing and turning for an hour, I concluded that sleep would not be mine until I took care of business. I spent a couple hours typing out the core concepts of all nine chapters in this book as well as the book title before I called it a night. Many of these ideas I had noted in the back of my Bible as ideas for separate magazine articles or books. Only now did they come together as a single project. Many times, I have cursed my chair for afflicting me so; at this time of completion, I bless him.

I thank Arthur Kelly, Joe Allison, and Stephen Lewis at Church of God Ministries, Inc., for their enthusiastic response to the book idea. Publication of such a work is an act of courage on their part. But this book had to be published by Warner Press and Church of God Ministries, Inc. No other publisher would be in such a position to address these issues. Had I written for another publisher, surely I would have had to write a very different book.

My colleagues at Warner Pacific College have been most gracious in receiving and supporting this pastor and novice professor. Parts of this book have been shaped by conversation with fellow members of the faculty. I thank President Jay Barber, Dr. John Hawthorne, and Dr. Steve Carver for extending an invitation to this unacclaimed pastor. I cannot imagine having such an opportunity to teach practical ministry anywhere else. I thank Dr. Connie Philips, Professor Megan Enos, Dr. Steve Lewis, Dr. Pam Plimpton, Dr. David Terrell, Professor Jeralynn Hawthorne, and Dr. Dennis Plies for their critiques of my chapter drafts. The fine library staff not only maintains the resources that supported my research, but Karla Castle and Cedate Schultz were helpful in finding information and editorial proofreading.

I would not be so remiss as to neglect a word of thanks to my parents, Ed and Vaughn Hickson. They did as much as anyone to shape my Christian faith from the earliest age. They stepped in to finance my education when my savings from teen jobs was exhausted and years later when I returned to academic studies while pastoring small churches with limited budgets for continuing education. As I wrote this book, they provided critique along the way. My parents should not be blamed for the content of the book; there are points of view in this book with which they do not agree. They did the best they could to steer their son in the right direction.

I thank God for his forbearance with me and the congregations of the Church of God that have provided me with a home over the years. This book, with all its criticisms, is my gift of love for you.

Introduction

WE CHURCH of God people have always sought the truth. Unfortunately, our devotion to the unity of God's church has sometimes led us to assume that beliefs of other traditions could be assimilated with our own. In our pursuit of holiness, we have migrated from sound doctrine to extremism—at times, to denial. Some of us have questioned longstanding teachings on the book of Revelation, and others have eagerly adopted end-time beliefs entirely foreign to our heritage. The movement that sought to include all Christian believers in one family now struggles with differences in race, culture, and theology. Where we once looked askance at medical science and sought healing only through prayer, we now rely on technology and drugs for our deliverance, like most American Christians, and even believe it immoral to do otherwise. Something has changed. The Church of God is becoming more like its neighbors.

Richard Foster suggests that Christian spirituality has developed as six traditions, each emphasizing certain themes: Contemplative, Holiness, Charismatic, Social Justice, Evangelical, and Incarnational.

The Contemplative stream offers lessons in the prayer-filled life. The Holiness stream emphasizes transformation of personal morality. The Charismatic tradition looks for the Holy Spirit to work in the contemporary community. The Social Justice tradition displays compassion through a lifestyle of service. The Evangelical tradition focuses on the Bible as the center of Christian life. The Incarnational tradition reminds us of the presence of God through rites of worship and engagement with the common acts of life.[1] Most Christians follow a blend of more than one tradition. The Church of God heritage is most at home in the Holiness tradition, with some influence from the Evangelical tradition, and a sprinkling of the Charismatic tradition.

---

1. Foster, *Streams of Living Water.*

While the Church of God shares common ground with the evangelical movement, some evangelical values conflict with Church of God heritage. While the Church of God has always been a holiness people, most evangelicals teach predestination and some form of eternal security ("once saved, always saved"). While Church of God spirituality is based on experience instead of creeds, evangelical theology is based on propositional doctrines. While the Church of God has always held an amillennial eschatology, most evangelicals hold premillennial expectations. While the Church of God has always understood that God calls women as well as men to ministry, many evangelicals are convinced that only men are called of God to be pastors of churches. This book is written to discuss ways in which Church of God beliefs are distinctive from those of evangelicals. Despite all the ways in which we agree, the Church of God does not fit well in the evangelical stream of Christianity.

In recent decades, evangelical beliefs have made significant inroads into the Church of God. Many Church of God people are reading Left Behind books with no comprehension that these take a very different approach to the book of Revelation and the last days than taken by the Church of God. Many Church of God people accept evangelical arguments against the ordination of women into ministry and have at times changed congregational bylaws to prevent their churches from hiring women. Church of God people have at times bought into evangelical propaganda that a refusal to use medical technology to delay death constitutes murder, as argued by evangelical groups like Focus on the Family and Operation Rescue.

The title of this book presents a double entendre: "Are you sure you're right?" On one hand, I am asking, "Are you sure that you are a part of the Christian Right?" The Church of God has not historically identified with that group of Christians. Rather than the extreme right wing (theologically and politically), the Church of God has occupied a more centrist position. But in recent decades, many Church of God people have been attracted to the messages presented by evangelical leaders like James Dobson, Pat Robertson, Tim LaHaye, and Charles Colson.

These ideas contrast with the writings of the Church of God heritage by Frederick G. Smith, Russell R. Byrum, Albert F. Gray, Gilbert W. Stafford, and others. Some will continue to identify with the teachings of modern evangelical leaders, even after their teachings are shown to differ with teachings from the Church of God heritage. To these people, I address the other side of the question: "Are you sure that your beliefs are correct?" To this end, I propose to use Scripture and reason to argue that we can do better than follow every wind of evangelical doctrine.

I expect that some will interpret this book as the product of a liberal agenda. *Liberal* and *conservative* are labels whose meaning varies and whose use offers little in terms of understanding. At times, it seems that we engage in bidding contests to outdo each other in our extremity. We need to understand that there are more than just the two choices of right and wrong. Truth is not necessarily found in the most extreme conservative position. However, to reject the Christian Right is not to be a liberal. If I must use these labels, I would describe myself to be a moderate leaning to the right. I believe that my position is biblical and fully consistent with the historical beliefs of the Church of God. This book is offered in hopes of calling my brothers and sisters in the Church of God back to our own heritage. Instead of seeking extremism, we must join together in a pursuit of holiness orthodoxy. Since the label *conservative* usually implies holding onto tradition, this book is truly a conservative effort, even if it will rankle some of my friends who count themselves as ultraconservatives. Could it be that those who are drifting from their Church of God heritage to evangelical doctrines are the true liberals? Instead of trying to imitate the beliefs and practices of denominational Christianity, we need to work from the foundation that has always grounded the Church of God.

Those of us who have long been a part of the Church of God are in danger of losing sight of the wonderful heritage given to us. We are prone to feelings of inferiority when we compare our own ministries with those of denominations or parachurch organizations. At times, we are embarrassed by the mistakes and failures of our own leaders. I humbly contend that we need to stop apologizing for who we are (or are not) and start proclaiming truth to the church The Church of God offers a message of divine truth that corrects the errors of the Christian Right.

A word of explanation is in order about the author. I grew up in Church of God congregations and earned my first degrees at a Church of God college. Aside from an eighteen-month stint as youth director at a United Methodist church while in seminary and two years with a Wesleyan church following a failed effort to plant a Church of God congregation in my native area, my entire ministry has been with the Church of God. It is my great privilege to teach ministry at Warner Pacific College, our college in the Pacific Northwest. If you cut me, I bleed Church of God. I love my heritage, warts and all. I am also a product of Dallas, Texas, often described as "the buckle of the Bible Belt." I know what it is to be a stranger in a strange land where most have never heard of the Church of God and where the terms *Christian* and *evangelical* are thought to be synonymous. Most churches in Texas are Baptist or Bible churches. I grew up in the shadow of Dallas Theological Seminary, a leading evangelical institution and the fountainhead of dispensational premillennialism.[2] My home church was influenced by groups holding values quite different from those of the Church of God, leading to the alienation of some individuals who had long been part of that congregation. As I have ministered in congregations across this country, I have seen indications that many in the Church of God have lost sight of our heritage. I offer this effort in hopes of introducing or reacquainting people with our own beliefs.

So I invite you to join me in a journey through some areas of contention. I will discuss a variety of issues in which I perceive that we are losing our heritage in a drift to evangelicalism.[3] Where possible, I will quote from some of our best theologians. I will discuss some of the relevant Bible texts and the ways those texts have been interpreted by the Church of God or by evangelicals. At times, I will have to make my

---

2. As in *Left Behind*. Chapter 3 is devoted to end-times beliefs.

3. If more explanation is needed, I offer two appendices: "What Is the Church of God?" and "What Is an Evangelical?"

points from other sources. I suspect that no one will agree with every argument I make. But I hope to challenge your thinking and provoke a revival of Church of God vision and energy. Thank you for coming along.

Jerry Hickson
Portland, Oregon

1.

Does the Bible Have a Greater Threat than the Thumper?

I WAS CANDIDATING to be the pastor of First Church of God in Kissimmee, Florida. I was thirty-two years old and had served as pastor of a church of similar size in California. During the candidating process, a potential pastor seeks to understand the congregation while the congregation also checks out the pastor. This intimidating process sometimes leads to unfortunate matches and short pastorates. But this particular weekend would result in the decision to begin what became the longest pastoral tenure of my career.

One of the people who participated in the scrutiny of this young pastor was Pastor Bob Hurt. Pastor Hurt had reason for his interest: He had founded the church twenty years earlier and had recently come out of retirement to serve as interim pastor. The church had forced the termination of the previous two pastors, so anxieties were understandably high. Pastor Hurt wanted one issue settled as we sat alone in the pastor's study: "What is your position on the inspiration of the Bible?" This is a significant question at any time and especially following the publication of "The Chicago Statement on Biblical Inerrancy" and Harold Lindsell's best-selling book, *The Battle for the Bible*. I had made this matter an area of personal research while in seminary. I was convinced that those who argued for biblical inerrancy had the best of intentions but presented a serious threat to the integrity of Holy Scripture. I explained my views to Pastor Hurt (as I will also do in this chapter with you). He responded by saying, "You believe in the Bible more than I do!"

While Pastor Hurt was exaggerating, I want to begin by assuring you that I love the Bible. I have loved the Bible all my life. Of all the spiritual disciplines, the practice I find the least difficult is reading my Bible. I have been reading the entire Bible each year for over fifteen years. I believe that the Bible is the uniquely inspired Word of God. No book equals the Holy Bible. Any teaching worthy of the label *Christian* must be grounded in this revelation.

While others exceed my Bible scholarship, I have pursued enough study to recognize that scholars have raised serious questions about this great book. These questions arose with remarkable vigor in the nineteenth century. Some scholars even rejected the Bible as a divine document. In response to such views, a Christian movement arose seeking to protect the Bible by asserting basic (or "fundamental") convictions that they believed must be held to preserve the Bible and the Christian faith. This group came to be known as *Fundamentalists*. Later, some chose to modify their convictions and preferred the label *Evangelicals*.[1] (Discussions about the accuracy and authority of Scripture are often described as a battle between liberals and conservatives, but it's important to realize that conservative Christians are not all alike.)

One conservative tactic in this battle is to describe the Bible as "inerrant." In order to protect the Bible from liberal criticism, some Christians assert that the Bible is without error in all that it states. In its purest form, *inerrancy* means that anything that the Bible states must be historically and scientifically accurate. A number of scriptural passages raise difficulties, as they seem to contradict one another in matters of chronology or measurement. Harold Lindsell and others have gone to great lengths to explain away all of the apparent contradictions. They seem to believe that if any contradiction can be found, the Bible falls flat as a document worthy of faith.

A modification of this tactic, designed to preclude this disastrous outcome, is to assert that the Bible is "inerrant in the original autographs." With this proviso, some believe they are protected against any

---

1. The five fundamentals were (1) the inerrancy of the Bible, (2) the virgin birth, (3) the substitutionary atonement, (4) the bodily resurrection of Jesus, and (5) the second coming (premillenial). Evangelicals continue to hold these fundamentals (sometimes adapting one or more). A key difference between fundamentalists and evangelicals is the desire to renounce separatism and engage in dialogue.

contradictions that cannot be explained away. They can assert that any discrepancy in Scripture was caused by copyists' errors.[2] They then can make some assumptions about what the original manuscript must have said.

Those who pose this argument overlook that fact that it concedes that we are far removed from the supposedly inerrant text. If we accept this argument, then we must admit that the Bibles we carry are no more than defective copies. If the spiritual authority of Scripture is based upon its factual accuracy, then no Bibles available to us have much authority.[3] Such outcomes destroy the usefulness of the Bible. We deny the authority of the Bible if we believe inerrancy is the proof of its authority.

I believe that the inerrancy argument presents a greater threat to the Bible than any other. While trying to protect the Bible from the attacks of liberal critics, the inerrantist holds the Bible hostage to the first factual error that is discovered. If the critic can find one contradiction, then the Bible gets cast on the dung heap of human history, with no credibility whatsoever. Any military tactician knows that the choice of battleground largely determines the outcome of a battle. The Battle of Gettysburg became a great defeat for the Confederacy because Lee advanced his troops against an entrenched opponent with strong artillery support on higher ground. Likewise, in the battle for the Bible, we are foolish to set the rules in such a way that the Bible will easily be invalidated.

The inerrancy argument is a rather recent development. The current campaign for inerrancy began in the 1970s. "The Chicago Statement on Inerrancy" was the result of a conference of a select group of Christians. Among the nineteen articles is the statement, "The authority

---

2. Before the invention of the printing press, all books were copied by hand. One scribe would read the text while one or more scribes carefully wrote what they heard. This process would easily result in misspellings and other errors. In some cases, it appears that scribes added commentary, probably in the margins. When a later reader used such a copy, content was easily copied from the margins into the main body of the text.

3. Inerrantists recognize this logical problem and respond by asserting that our copies communicate enough of the Word of God to be valid.

of Scripture is inescapably impaired if this total divine inerrancy is in any way limited." The statement goes on to assert "confession of the full authority, infallibility and inerrancy of Scripture is vital to a sound understanding of the whole of the Christian faith."[4] The popular interest in inerrancy is rooted in the publication of a book by Harold Lindsell, former faculty member of Fuller Theological Seminary, protesting the shift of that school from fundamentalism to moderate Christianity. These efforts looked back to the teachings of the old Princeton school. In the mid-nineteenth century, Princeton was far more conservative than the university we know today. B.B. Warfield, Charles Hodge, and A.A. Hodge were leading authorities in this Princeton theology, which eventually became known as fundamentalism. While most modern evangelicals would not identify themselves as fundamentalists, they share this fundamentalist heritage of Princeton theology.

In his 1976 book, *The Battle for the Bible,* Lindsell pressed the Princeton theology to its logical conclusion, making inerrancy a watershed issue in Protestant theological dialogue. Lindsell asserted, "The authors of Scripture, under the guidance of the Holy Spirit, were preserved from making factual, historical, scientific, or other errors."[5] Lindsell insisted that any denial of inerrancy would lead to a denial of other cardinal Christian doctrines. Lindsell did not advocate a doctrine of mechanical dictation (i.e., that God dictated Scripture verbatim to the biblical writers), but he insisted that the orthodox Christian doctrine of the inspiration of the Bible is founded upon the idea of inerrancy.[6]

Biblical inerrancy grew out of a philosophy that has been dominant in Western culture for the last two centuries. This philosophy is variously labeled rationalism, Scottish realism, or common sense. This school of thought insists that truths are concrete and definable. Words can be trusted to accurately portray all realities. This mindset is characteristic of the modern era in Europe, the United States, and other places where

---

4. "Chicago Statement on Biblical Inerrancy."

5. Lindsell, *Battle for the Bible*, 31.

6. Ibid., 32–33.

it became dominant.[7] In the later decades of the twentieth century, the mindset of modernism was found lacking and has increasingly been supplanted by a worldview labeled *postmodern.*

A careful study of the nature of language and its meaning (linguistics) will show that rationalism, while simple and attractive, does not describe the world in which we live. A word does not "mean what it means." Meaning resides with the one who sends the message.[8] When we are uncertain about the meaning of a message, we might find a clue in the dictionary, but we will do better to go to the messenger to ask what was meant. In the case of the Bible, the ancient writers are no longer with us to clarify their intent. We must therefore study the context of each word and other uses of the same word (preferably by the same writer) to understand what was intended. Dr. Lindsell and other evangelicals of his persuasion betray their dependence upon the discredited common-sense worldview by asserting, "Words have specific meanings."[9]

The inerrantist argues that since the word *inspiration* means "God-breathed," if we affirm that the Bible is "inspired" we must affirm that the Bible is written by God. This point of view ranges from the extreme dictation theory (that God dictated every word of Scripture to Moses, David, Paul, and the other writers) to various accommodations to human participation in the inspiration process. Inerrantists assert that since "God cannot lie,"[10] everything stated in the Bible must be factually accurate.

The doctrine of inerrancy has become a litmus test by which evangelicals[11] define Christian orthodoxy. One must not only affirm the

---

7. An excellent survey of this is offered by Rogers and McKim, *Authority and Inspiration of the Bible.*

8. DeVito, *Messages,* 96–97.

9. Lindsell, *Battle for the Bible,* 33.

10. "The Holy Spirit by nature cannot lie." (Lindsell, *Battle for the Bible,* 31.) I have heard Lindsell use the statement "God cannot lie" in a recording of one of his speeches. Lindsell was making reference to Hebrews 6:18.

11. I am using *evangelical* in a restricted sense, as explained in the Introduction and Appendix B.

inspiration and authority of the Bible, one is required to use the word *inerrancy* to be judged faithful to Christianity. Among some evangelicals, this verges on becoming a creed, and creedalism has always been foreign to the Church of God. The emphasis on the use of a particular word as a test of evangelical loyalty is reminiscent of the Israelites' use of *shibboleth*.[12]

What has been said about inerrancy in Church of God heritage? A sampling of key writings will show that Church of God writers have not mentioned inerrancy in discussing the inspiration of the Bible.[13] While Lindsell and others believe that we must cling to inerrancy in order to defend the Bible from skeptics, such a concern cannot be found in Church of God writings. This is not to suggest that the Church of God has a low regard for the inspiration of Scripture. As one of our classic songs proclaims, "The Bible is our rule of faith."[14] And as Church of God historian Merle Strege says, "Early movement writers made few explicit statements concerning the inspiration of the Bible. Its authority and inspiration were undisputed."[15]

> The Church of God movement was not heavily invested in
> the Fundamentalist Controversy of the 1920s. The saints
> were quite aware of that debate, but they remained aloof for
> two reasons. First, they generally regarded it as an intramural
> struggle of denominational Christianity; as such it was merely
> a Babylonish squabble. Secondly and more important, how-
> ever, there was nothing in the Church of God movement's
> teaching on biblical inspiration and authority that gave them
> reason to enter the Fundamentalist fray. While it is very diffi-

---

12. In Judges 12, a battle tactic was to force combatants to pronounce the word to determine whether they were of the right tribe. After I wrote this, I was surprised to find that J. I. Packer agrees that inerrancy is a shibboleth. Packer thinks this is a good thing! See Packer, "Lamp in a Dark Place," 24–25.

13. I recognize the weakness of an argument from silence. Still, it is significant that Church of God writers place so little emphasis on a word that evangelicals insist is key to the definition of biblical authority.

14. Naylor, "The Church's Jubilee."

15. Strege, *I Saw the Church*, 228.

cult to state the convictions of the grassroots movement, it is quite clear that published writers such as H. C. Wickersham (1850-1916) and Russell Byrum, whose lives spanned a period from the first to third generations of movement leadership, both taught a doctrine of inspiration that focused on the Bible's writers before its words or even its ideas.[16]

Many have held that the classic book of Church of God doctrine is F. G. Smith's *What the Bible Teaches*. Smith devotes his preliminary to "The Divine Authority of the Scriptures." In the first sentence, Smith says that "the divine authority of the Holy Scriptures is accepted presumptively." Although Smith lists evidences for the authority of the Bible, he never mentions inerrancy.[17]

The first systematic theology text written in the Church of God was *Christian Theology* by R. R. Byrum. Though he does not use the word *inerrancy*, Byrum directly renounces the idea that God dictated the words of Scripture.[18] Byrum does make the point that all parts of the Bible are inspired, even if all parts are not equally important.[19] Describing the mystery of the Bible's composition, Byrum says, "The Scriptures are a result of the interworking of the human and the divine, not of one without the other."[20] Byrum devotes five pages to allegations of errors in the Bible and seeks to show that such claims are baseless. At one point, he also speaks of the "original manuscripts."[21] At these moments, he seems to engage in the same thought processes as the inerrantists. Yet he follows each of these statements with a declaration that inerrancy is not the basis of biblical authority. "If the critics could

---

16. Ibid., 227–28.

17. Evidences listed by Smith include (1) the unity of the Bible, (2) the prophecies of the Bible, (3) the moral beauty of the Bible, (4) the simplicity of the Bible, (5) transformation of character, and (6) claims of divine authorship; Smith, *What the Bible Teaches*, 15–22.

18. Even Lindsell disclaims the idea of dictation. But at the grassroots level, it is difficult to see a difference between what many mean by inerrancy and manual dictation.

19. Byrum, *Christian Theology*, 170–71.

20. Ibid., 171.

21. Ibid., 173.

actually prove that the original manuscripts of the Bible contain errors, it would not disprove divine inspiration, but would merely require many believers in inspiration to allow a larger place for the human element."[22] "Even if the Bible were convicted of error in secular matters the inspiration of its religious message would not necessarily be affected."[23] In a 1921 article in *Gospel Trumpet*, Byrum wrote, "The bulk of the Bible was given by God through men" and "the true theory [of inspiration] must allow both the human and the divine element in the producing of the Bible."[24]

A. F. Gray addressed "The Inspiration of the Scriptures" early in his *Christian Theology*. He not only disclaims the concept of dictation but goes on to describe verbal inspiration as "a defenseless position." Gray says, "It is better to allow that the human element in the Bible is really human and that the writers are responsible for it." Gray makes the point that the Bible is written with less exactitude than the inerrantist perceives. "It is one thing to believe that God gave a vital truth to his servant and allowed him to express it in his own way and quite another to believe that God chose the exact language in which that truth was to be expressed." "Divine perfection should not be expected in a book that is partly human."[25]

A more recent statement of Church of God beliefs is *Theology for Disciples,* by Gilbert W. Stafford. Though he does not use the word *inerrancy*, Stafford lists three classic approaches to describing biblical inspiration, including "dynamic inspiration." The idea here is that it was neither the words themselves nor even the message that was inspired, but rather the writers were inspired through their relationship with God.[26] What Stafford calls "dynamic inspiration" was described as early as 1894 by H.C. Wickersham.

---

22. Ibid., 172–73.

23. Ibid., 176.

24. Byrum, "How Did God Inspire the Bible?" 4–5.

25. Gray, *Christian Theology*, 1:76–80.

26. Stafford, *Theology for Disciples*, 47–49.

The different writers of the books of the Bible were inspired of God. It is not the words of the Bible that were inspired, it is not the thoughts of the Bible that were inspired; it is the men who wrote the Bible that were inspired. Inspiration acts not on the man's words, not on the man's thoughts, but on the man himself; so that he, by his own spontaneity, under the impulse of the Holy Ghost, conceives certain thoughts and gives utterance to them in certain words, both the words and the thoughts receiving the peculiar impress of the mind which conceived and uttered them.[27]

Wickersham also discusses how different the Bible would be if God had chosen the words.

Stafford goes on to list four types of evidence that the Bible is Scripture.

In short, the Christian scripture principle is that those writings are scripture that are:

1. experienced by the church at large as being inspired by God,
2. accepted by the church at large as being sacred writings,
3. instructive for salvation through faith in Jesus Christ, and
4. useful for the purpose of instructing, judging, aligning, and shaping the people of God so that they will come to be and do what God wants them to be and do.[28]

The Church of God General Assembly addressed the issue of biblical inspiration in 1981 without advocating use of the word *inerrancy*. The closest their statement came to inerrancy was to say that the Bible is "without error in all that it affirms."[29] This is a common caveat, which seems to satisfy some people who are concerned about an erosion of confidence in biblical authority without completely endorsing the inerrancy argument.

---

27. Wickersham, *Holiness Bible Subject*, 18–19.

28. Stafford, *Theology for Disciples*, 52.

29. Callen, *Following the Light*, 203–4.

Those who promote inerrancy as a vital doctrine are generally from traditions other than the Church of God. Often, these persons come from the Reformed tradition, with a theology that is far more deterministic than that of the Church of God.[30] The Church of God has always held a high view of the Bible as Holy Scripture. We have not seen a need to use the word *inerrancy* to describe the authority of the Bible. In a book review on *The Battle for the Bible*, the Church of God (Anderson, IN) was cited along with the Church of the Nazarene as leaders in the effort to counter the campaign for inerrancy by the National Association of Evangelicals and the Evangelical Theological Society.[31]

While I affirm the divine authorship of Scripture, I believe the inerrancy argument distorts the true nature of the Bible. The doctrine of biblical inspiration has a duality not unlike the doctrine of christology. Just as Jesus was "fully God yet fully man,"[32] so the Bible is God-breathed yet humanly written. This dialectical tension upholds the divine authority of the Bible while recognizing that the humanity of the writers limited what they could write. All Scripture is written within a historical and cultural context. Those who wrote the words were not overpowered by God to write things that were beyond their worldview. Acceptance of this reality provides a framework for grappling with many of the problem texts in the Bible. God never lies, but the Bible must be read within its historical context. Part of that context was the worldview of ancient cultures.

If the credibility of the Bible is destroyed by the first proven contradiction, then we need go no further than the accounts of the temptation of Jesus to end the discussion. We find these accounts in the fourth chapters of the gospels of Matthew and Luke. In each case, Satan tempts Jesus three times after the Lord had fasted for a long time. Each account portrays the first temptation as Satan challenging Jesus to turn stones into bread to satiate his hunger. But we find a discrepancy in what happens next. In Matthew, the narrative says that Jesus was

---

30. See chapter two for a discussion of the Church of God and determinism.

31. Dayton, "Battle for the Bible," 978.

32. A popular paraphrase of the Chalcedonian Creed.

then tempted to throw himself from the pinnacle of the temple as a display of his divine power and protection. Then Jesus was tempted to bow to Satan in a bargain for all the kingdoms of the world. In Luke, the order of the second and third temptations is reversed. Which is accurate? Was Jesus tempted to (A) turn stones into bread, (B) jump from the Temple, and (C) bow down to Satan? Or was it A, then C, then B? If getting the chronology correct is proof of the Bible's veracity, then it fails in this simple instance.[33] The inerrantist says, "It doesn't matter which is the correct order." To which I respond, "Precisely!" Precision in chronology or measurement was not the purpose of scriptural teaching.[34] Expecting such of the Bible imposes modern expectations on ancient writers.

Far better to claim for the Bible the authority it claims for itself. *Inerrancy* is a modern concept foreign to the Bible. The Bible says that it is *inspired*. Inerrantists deduce that *inspired* means "inerrant." Yet the Bible never claims to be without error, nor does it base its authority on its own accuracy of detail. We should not impose on the Bible a modern standard that was irrelevant to the writers of Scripture.

I am not arguing that the Bible is full of errors. I am saying that we should not base the Bible's authority on the claim of inerrancy.

Rather, we must assert that the authority of Scripture is proven by its life-changing power. The Bible is authoritative because it testifies to Christ. Through the pages of the written Word, we are confronted with the living Word. No other book has this life-giving power.

---

33. While inerrantists love to insist that there are no contradictions in the Bible, other examples can be cited. How did King Saul meet his death? (Compare 1 Samuel 31 with 2 Samuel 1.) How did Judas commit suicide? (Compare Matthew 27:5 with Acts 1:18–19.) Great efforts have been made to harmonize such discrepancies. Another approach is to accept them as the result of multiple authors.

34. Lindsell concedes this point when explaining how a head count can be 23,000 in one place and 24,000 in another. Then he engages is geometric gymnastics to explain away the measurement of the molten sea. He concedes the point in responding to Jesus' statement that the mustard seed is the smallest of seeds but computes two passages to produce an account of Peter denying Jesus six times! See Lindsell, *Battle for the Bible*, 161–76.

What we are facing here is a paradox—two truths that seem to be in conflict. The Bible is the divinely inspired Word of God, yet the Bible is a collection of documents written by a variety of human individuals over several centuries. As is often the case with paradox, truth is found in the tension between them.[35] We must not allow either aspect of the Bible's character to diminish the other. If we deny the divine element, the Bible becomes merely a collection of ancient stories and ideas. If we deny the human element, the Bible becomes a false idol that will inevitably be toppled.

Ironically, evangelicals share with the Church of God a conviction that the Bible is the sole source of authority for Christian belief and life. Evangelicals stand on the principle of *sola scriptura* (Scripture only), and the Church of God declares, "We have no creed but the Bible." Our common devotion to the Bible is one our similarities. We differ in how we choose to honor Holy Writ.

Recent history demonstrates that one is required to affirm inerrancy to be an evangelical. However, one does not have to believe in inerrancy to be a Christian. Contrary to the opinion of some, many Christians do not believe in biblical inerrancy. Inerrancy is a concept that is foreign to Church of God heritage.

For Further Study

Byrum, Russell R. *Christian Theology*. Anderson, IN: Gospel Trumpet Company, 1925. See "Part Two: Evidences of Divine Revelation, or Apologetics."

Gray, Albert F. *Christian Theology*. Anderson, IN: Gospel Trumpet Company, 1944.1:39-108.

Stafford, Gilbert W. *Theology for Disciples*. Anderson, IN: Warner Press, 1996. See chap. 3, "The Church's Book of Faith."

"Chicago Statement on Biblical Inerrancy." *Journal of the Evangelical Theological Society*, December 21, 1978, 289–296.

---

35. I must credit Dr. Barry Callen for this concept taken from a paper he presented while my seminary dean.

Lindsell, Harold. *The Battle for the Bible.* Grand Rapids, MI: Zondervan, 1976.

Dayton, Donald W. "The Battle for the Bible." *Christian Century,* November 10, 1976, 976–80.

Rogers, Jack, ed. *Biblical Authority.* Waco, TX: Word, 1977.

Rogers, Jack B., and Donald K. McKim. *The Authority and Inspiration of the Bible.* New York: Harper & Row, 1979.

QUESTIONS FOR DISCUSSION

1. Do you believe that we must assert the inerrancy of Scripture in order to claim the inspiration of the Bible? Why or why not?

2. Do you agree with Hickson's charge that inerrancy has become a matter of evangelical creed which contradicts the traditional teaching of the Church of God? Why or why not?

3. How do you explain the apparent discrepancies in the Bible?

4. What do you think of the argument that the writers of the Bible were inspired (dynamic inspiration), but not the words themselves?

5. How do you describe the authority and inspiration of the Bible?

2.

Does the Sovereignty of God Preclude Our Free Will?

ROGER WAS sitting outside the barn-like auditorium used for the worship service earlier that evening. He had come to this youth camp with a friend who attended another church in town. Roger was feeling very much out of place after hearing four days of Bible teaching that differed greatly from what he had learned. Now he was in a rather heated discussion with some of the other guys from his cabin. "I believe that we are saved by grace," said Roger, "but I just don't see why the preacher makes it sound like my faith doesn't matter."

"But that's what the Bible says!" countered Kurt and Brian.

"The whole idea is that God chose us, we didn't choose him!" said his friend Brian.

"I don't know," demurred Roger, "I always understood that we have to respond to God in faith. And I have trouble with the idea that how I live doesn't make any difference if I am saved."

"Sure, it makes a difference," protests Dan, "but it's like Mr. Galen said the other morning: Once you are adopted by God, you can never be unadopted." The others chimed in their agreement.

"And I don't get all the talk in that other conference about Israel!" Roger continued. "What about it don't you understand?" asked Kurt, "Like the Bible says, God has guaranteed that a descendant of David has to rule in Jerusalem, and God will keep that promise in the last day. We know that is about to happen since God has reestablished the nation of Israel."

By now, Roger's brain was getting really tired. He wondered if maybe he should call his parents and go home. If only he could talk this over with his youth pastor.

One of the great dividing points for Christians is the debate between Calvinists and Arminians. Many American churches profess a heritage that goes back to the sixteenth-century century theologian John Calvin. While Calvin is highly regarded by the Church of God, too, we have a different theological heritage going back to the Dutch professor Jacobus Arminius. Arminian theology arises from five basic convictions concerning salvation: (1) conditional election, (2) universal redemption, (3) moral freedom, (4) resistibility of grace, and (5) possibility of apostasy.[1] In response to these, the Synod of Dort established the now famous TULIP or five-point Calvinism: (1) total depravity, (2) unconditional election, (3) limited atonement, (4) irresistible grace, and (5) perseverence of the saints.

While Calvinism presents a complex system of nuanced theology, the idea commonly gets reduced to the statement "Once saved always saved" or the label *eternal security*. Calvinism asserts that God decides who will be saved and who will not, and whatever God says goes. At issue here is more than just a theology of salvation. The underlying doctrine is divine sovereignty. So any denial of these beliefs is perceived as a rejection of the sovereignty of God. Not only does this affect doctrine about salvation, but it also informs a system of beliefs about what will happen at the end of time. The Calvinist approach to divine sovereignty also influences what many Christians believe about suffering. The overarching principle in all of these discussions is *determinism*, the idea that God controls all things. But is that true?

A determinist says that God elects those who are saved. In other words, God chooses whose sins will be forgiven. People are brought in to the kingdom of God not by their decision but by God's choice alone. Some determinists even contend that God chooses who will be left out of his eternal kingdom (double predestination). This doctrine argues that those predestined to damnation deserve to be left out, since all have sinned and God's grace extends only to those whom God has chosen.

In contrast, the Church of God is among those who believe that God's grace is extended to "whoever will believe" (John 3:18; Rom 10:9). The

---

1. Byrum, *Christian Theology*, 342, 406.

Bible indicates that we must all make a choice concerning God. If salvation comes only by God's election, then evangelism and missions are pointless. Why, then, do churches that preach election often have altar calls? (Ironically, many churches that profess to be Calvinist in doctrine are Arminian in practice.)

The determinist also says that Christians are unable to lose their salvation. Since Christians cannot find salvation in the first place, the conclusion follows that nothing we can do will remove us from the salvation that God has given. Otherwise, God would be inconsistent. When someone professes faith in Christ and does not live in holiness, a determinist says they may be out of fellowship with God, but their eternal destiny remains fixed. Many churches have bus ministries based on this idea of eternal security; they feel compelled to bring children in, so that they will pray the prayer that will fix their eternal destiny. Discipleship tends to be less significant in congregations where eternal security is taught. The word *backsliding* is foreign in a determinist context. A person whom we might call backslidden is said by others never to have known Christ. This position overlooks the fact that the Bible speaks of backsliding from faith. God said to the nation of Israel through the prophet Jeremiah, "You have rejected me, you keep on backsliding. So I will lay hands on you and destroy you; I can no longer show compassion" (Jer 15:6). Clearly, this offers us an example of people who once knew the Lord and then lost their salvation.

The determinist says that God's covenant is unconditional. Even though biblical scholars have demonstrated the mutuality of covenants in the ancient world, the determinist insists that God establishes the parameters of his covenants unilaterally. Because of this, determinists teach that God owes something to the nation of Israel. The argument holds that some blessings which God has promised to Israel have not taken place. Therefore, God must restore Israel before history ends to complete his plan. This explains why some Christians get so excited about news concerning the modern-day nation of Israel. (We will look further at this phenomenon in chapter three.) But the Bible repeatedly presents God's covenant as conditional. With a few exceptions, God approaches his people with an if-then offer.[2] When Israel failed to keep the covenant, God did not break his promises; he has kept all of the promises he made.[3] God's covenant is conditional and Israel failed to keep the conditions. The New Testament speaks of the church as "the New Israel" and warns that we will suffer the same fate as ancient Israel if we are not faithful (Rom 9:30–11:24.)

Determinists say that God ordains everything that happens to us. They believe that since God is sovereign, everything that happens is part of his plan. Determinist Christians reassure themselves and others with statements like, There must be a reason for this, or, I believe that everything has a purpose. Yet this belief can destroy a person's faith when life becomes cruel. What we are confronting here is the question of theodicy: Why does a loving and all-powerful God allow suffering?[4] Theodicy presents us again with a paradox: we cannot deny the love of God or the power of God or the reality of suffering. Some have tried to do each of these things, but biblical faith holds these truths in tension. The Westminster Confession states, "God from all eternity did by the most holy and wise counsel of his own free will freely and unchangeably ordain whatsoever comes to pass."[5] The Church of God stands among those who find the answer to theodicy in the reality of human free will. God in his sovereignty has granted us the power to make choices. Some of our choices bring painful consequences. God bears no responsibility for our evil or the suffering that results. Rather than blaming God, we should accept the fact that we live in a fallen world. Much of our suffering has nothing to do with any specific sin we have committed, yet we

---

2. Ex 19:5–6; Lev 26:23–24; Deut 28; 29:19–20; 30:17; 32:19; Judg 2:3; Josh 23:12–13; 24:20; 1 Sam 12:15, 25; 13:13–14; 2 Kings 23:3; 1 Chron 22:9; 2 Chron 27:17; 15:2; Neh 1:9; Ps 89; Isa 1:19–20; Jer 7:2, 23; 11:4–5; 12:7, 16–17; 15:6, 19; 17:4; 18:6–10; 22:5–30; 31:31–34; 32:37–41; 33:15–22; Lam 2:7; Ezek 33:12–16; Hos 2:4; 4:6; 9:15–17; 13:9; Amos 9:7; Zech. 11:10–11; Heb. 8:9.

3. Deut 28 is one place where we find both blessings and curses promised by God depending on how Israel responded to the covenant. The determinist wants to hold God to the blessings while ignoring the curses.

4. *Theodicy* is a word combining the Greek words for *God* and *justice*. Thus, theodicy is a defense of the justice of God.

5. Cited in Byrum, *Christian Theology*, 408.

suffer because we live in a world of people who have sinned. Theodicy is a complex matter that deserves a book in itself.[6]

One thing can be said for determinists: they are very logical. Their whole belief system is rooted in a logical syllogism that begins with the sovereignty of God. Certain Bible verses are used that buttress the conclusions reached by deductive reasoning. However, deductive reasoning can go astray if there is any flaw in the premises.[7] It is better to engage in inductive reasoning, which considers all of the evidence. While many Bible verses seem to confirm the beliefs of the determinist, the whole counsel of Scripture leads to other conclusions. Further, life is not always as logical as the determinist would imagine. Life is all too often irrational. We need a faith that is true to this reality.

Although determinism is foreign to the way the Church of God has understood the Bible and truth, any survey of Church of God literature will reveal a patchwork quilt of teachings on this point. Subtle references to all the beliefs of the determinist can be found in Church of God writings. However, mainstream Church of God doctrine refutes the teachings of determinism and eternal security. We believe that God has granted all persons free will. We believe that salvation is by grace through faith. We believe that a Christian's perseverance in the faith is a result of ongoing choices to be faithful. We believe that God's covenant has always been conditional, and that Israel has no separate plan of salvation apart from faith in Jesus Christ. We do not believe that every experience of suffering is ordained by God.

Gil Stafford makes the point that God did not create good and evil as two options from which we might choose. Everything that God creates is good. We have the option of choosing or rejecting the good that God offers us. "The origin of evil is a human invention; it is rooted in the human decision to transgress the prerogative knowledge and mysterious personhood of God."[8] Stafford concedes that the Wesleyan

---

6. I am writing such a book. My working title is *Surviving the Hard Side of Life*.

7. See Callen, *Faithful in the Meantime*, 77–81.

8. Stafford, *Theology for Disciples* , 272–74.

approach to sin and salvation "may not result in the most airtight logical system...but it does reflect the realistic dynamism of the Bible."[9]

The Church of God has always chosen the theology of Arminius and Wesley over the theology of John Calvin. Both Gilbert Stafford and A. F. Gray, leading Church of God theologians, discuss the Remonstrance of Arminius and the Synod of Dort.[10] After demonstrating the differences between Calvinism and Arminianism, A. F. Gray says, "Saving faith is exercised voluntarily."[11] While not denying the sovereignty of God, Church of God writers maintain a belief that God has given us free will.

R. R. Byrum discussed the issues related to determinism at several places in his classic textbook *Christian Theology*. Discussing salvation, he wrote, "Pardon is granted only through faith in Christ, who made the atonement."[12] Discussing the issue of free will, Byrum said, "If men's wills are determined, sin is not reprehensible and goodness deserves no reward."[13] He went on to explain at length how the fact that God has foreknowledge of all things does not mean that God determines all things.[14] In response to the argument that divine sovereignty implies divine control over all things, Byrum said, "We distinguish between the rule over things and the government of free beings. An efficient ruler in a civil government does not determine the wills of his subjects." He went on to say, "The determinist's theory amounts to reducing the subjects of God's government to the condition of machinery."[15]

When he discussed the various Christian theories of original sin, Byrum said, "Arminianism holds that the power to do good was lost through the fall, but that through divine grace it is restored so man can

---

9. Ibid., 306.

10. Ibid., 304–5; Gray, *Christian Theology*, 2:54–58.

11. Gray, *Christian Theology*, 2:70.

12. Byrum, *Christian Theology*, 145.

13. Ibid., 305.

14. Ibid., 311.

15. Ibid., 312.

choose to serve God or not."[16] Wesleyans describe God's restoration of our power of choice as "prevenient grace." Later, Byrum said, "The Scriptures very definitely represent forgiveness of sin as conditional."[17] When discussing the biblical concept of election, Byrum pointed out that Scripture used that word in a corporate sense to speak of the election of the nation of Israel or the election of the church, as opposed to the sense of individual election preferred by Calvinists.[18]

Gilbert Stafford addressed the issue of the kingdom of God in the 2004 Doctrinal Dialogue at the North American Conference of the Church of God. There, Stafford made a three-point refutation of the determinist concept that the covenant made by God with David was unconditional and irrevocable.

1. The promise of the Kingdom was given in the Old Testament to David and the prophet Nathan (see 2 Sam 5–7).
2. The fulfillment of this promise, however, was conditional on Israel's obedience to God (e.g., 1 Kings 9:1–9; 11:6–13).
3. Since Israel was disobedient, the promise was not fulfilled (e.g., Dan 9:4–19).[19]

The Bible repeatedly teaches that God's free gift of salvation requires a response of faith in order to be received. Jesus said, "Whoever believes and is baptized will be saved, but whoever does not believe will be condemned" (Mark 16:16). In his memorable statement to Nicodemus, Jesus said,

> For God so loved the world that he gave his one and only Son, that whoever believes in him shall not perish but have eternal life. For God did not send his Son into the world to condemn the world, but to save the world through him. Whoever believes in him is not condemned, but whoever does not believe

---

16. Ibid., 342.
17. Ibid., 398.
18. Ibid., 409.
19. Stafford, "Eschatology."

stands condemned already because he has not believed in the name of God's one and only Son. (John 3:16–18)

In setting forth the thesis of his epistle to the Romans, Paul said, "I am not ashamed of the gospel, because it is the power of God for the salvation of everyone who believes: first for the Jew, then for the Gentile" (1:16). In each of these texts, salvation demands a response. God surely offers salvation to us, but we are required to exercise faith. The argument that God unconditionally elects certain people for salvation overlooks these texts.

The Bible repeatedly speaks of people losing their faith and falling away from God. The prophet Azariah spoke the Word of the Lord to the king: "The LORD is with you when you are with him. If you seek him, he will be found by you, but if you forsake him, he will forsake you" (2 Chron 15:2). The prophet Isaiah spoke of God's response to the failure of Israel to keep the covenant, "They rebelled and grieved his Holy Spirit. So he turned and became their enemy and he himself fought against them" (Isa. 63:10). The prophet Jeremiah repeatedly confronts this issue. "This is what the LORD says: 'When men fall down, do they not get up? When a man turns away, does he not return? Why then have these people turned away? Why does Jerusalem always turn away? They cling to deceit; they refuse to return" (Jer 8:4-5). "Although our sins testify against us, O LORD, do something for the sake of your name. For our backsliding is great; we have sinned against you" (Jer 14:7). "Through your own fault you will lose the inheritance I gave you" (Jer 17:4a). Jeremiah would have made a poor Calvinist. I wonder if this is why the writings of Jeremiah are not studied as often as those of Isaiah. The prophet Ezekiel records this Word of the Lord: "I will save them from all their sinful backsliding, and I will cleanse them. They will be my people, and I will be their God" (Ezek 37:23).

As we move into the New Testament, we find Paul writing, "Consider therefore the kindness and sternness of God: sternness to those who fell, but kindness to you, provided that you continue in his kindness. Otherwise, you also will be cut off" (Rom 11:22). If Christians cannot fall away from grace, why does Hebrews include this warning:

"See to it, brothers, that none of you has a sinful, unbelieving heart that turns away from the living God" (3:12)? Hebrews also indicates that God's covenant with Israel was not unconditional: "It still remains that some will enter that rest, and those who formerly had the gospel preached to them did not go in, because of their disobedience" (4:6). The writer of Hebrews addressed believers when he said, "See to it that no one misses the grace of God" (12:15). James concludes his letter with this, "My brothers, if one of you should wander from the truth and someone should bring him back, remember this: Whoever turns a sinner from the error of his way will save him from death and cover over a multitude of sins" (5:19–20). Among the seven letters to the church in Revelation, we find this warning, "Yet I hold this against you: You have forsaken your first love. Remember the height from which you have fallen! Repent and do the things you did at first. If you do not repent, I will come to you and remove your lampstand from its place" (2:4–5). All of this biblical teaching conflicts with the doctrine that salvation is a permanent guarantee that cannot be lost.

Earlier, I listed several scriptures that describe God's covenant as conditional; let us look at some of them. On Mount Sinai, God said to Moses, "'Now if you obey me fully and keep my covenant, then out of all nations you will be my treasured possession. Although the whole earth is mine, you will be for me a kingdom of priests and a holy nation.' These are the words you are to speak to the Israelites" (Ex 19:5–6). The twenty-eighth chapter of Deuteronomy lists not only the blessings offered in God's covenant with Israel but also the curses for disobedience. Before entering the Promised Land, Joshua warned the nation, "If you forsake the LORD and serve foreign gods, he will turn and bring disaster on you and make an end of you, after he has been good to you" (Josh 24:20). Because of their failure to keep the covenant, the nation of Israel went into exile.

I suggested earlier that if more Christians would read the book of Jeremiah, there might be better understanding of the conditional nature of God's covenant. God speaks through the prophet, "I gave them (Israel) this command: Obey me, and I will be your God and you will be my people. Walk in all the ways I command you, that it may go well with you" (7:23). God reminds the prophet of "the terms I commanded your forefathers when I brought them out of Egypt, out of the iron-smelting furnace. I said, 'Obey me and do everything I command you, and you will be my people, and I will be your God. Then I will fulfill the oath I swore to your forefathers, to give them a land flowing with milk and honey'—the land you possess today" (11:4–5). God says, "I will forsake my house, abandon my inheritance; I will give the one I love into the hands of her enemies" (12:7). Even after sending his people into exile, God offers restoration, "If you repent, I will restore you that you may serve me" (15:19). Loss of the covenant does not diminish God's faithfulness: "Through your own fault you will lose the inheritance I gave you" (17:4).

With the image of the potter, God clearly communicated the conditionality of the covenant. "If at any time I announce that a nation or kingdom is to be uprooted, torn down and destroyed, and if that nation I warned repents of its evil, then I will relent and not inflict on it the disaster I had planned. And if at another time I announce that a nation or kingdom is to be built up and planted, and if it does evil in my sight and does not obey me, then I will reconsider the good I had intended to do for it" (Jer 18:6–10). The unbiased reader can clearly understand that Jeremiah speaks of the rejection of the covenant by Israel. In the twenty-second chapter of Jeremiah, God goes so far as to describe the end of the Davidic monarchy.

Jeremiah goes on to reveal the new covenant God is preparing. The message in Jeremiah 31:31–34 clearly indicates that the old covenant with Israel was to be replaced with a better covenant for all people:

> "The time is coming," declares the LORD, "when I will make a new covenant with the house of Israel and with the house of Judah. It will not be like the covenant I made with their forefathers when I took them by the hand to lead them out of Egypt, because they broke my covenant, though I was a husband to them," declares the LORD. "This is the covenant I will make with the house of Israel after that time," declares

the LORD. "I will put my law in their minds and write it on their hearts. I will be their God, and they will be my people. No longer will a man teach his neighbor, or a man his brother, saying, 'Know the LORD,' because they will all know me, from the least of them to the greatest," declares the LORD. "For I will forgive their wickedness and will remember their sins no more."[20]

God even said he would restore the nation of Israel after the exile if they would live in obedience to his covenant.

> I will surely gather them from all the lands where I banish them in my furious anger and great wrath; I will bring them back to this place and let them live in safety. They will be my people, and I will be their God. I will give them singleness of heart and action, so that they will always fear me for their own good and the good of their children after them. I will make an everlasting covenant with them: I will never stop doing good to them, and I will inspire them to fear me, so that they will never turn away from me. I will rejoice in doing them good and will assuredly plant them in this land with all my heart and soul. (Jer 32:37–41)

Jeremiah reveals how the covenant would be fulfilled in the coming of the Christ.

> "'In those days and at that time I will make a righteous Branch sprout from David's line; he will do what is just and right in the land. In those days Judah will be saved and Jerusalem will live in safety. This is the name by which it will be called: The LORD Our Righteousness.'

---

20. This passage from Jeremiah is quoted in Hebrews 8:8–12.

For this is what the LORD says: 'David will never fail to have a man to sit on the throne of the house of Israel, nor will the priests, who are Levites, ever fail to have a man to stand before me continually to offer burnt offerings, to burn grain offerings and to present sacrifices.'"

The word of the LORD came to Jeremiah: "This is what the LORD says: 'If you can break my covenant with the day and my covenant with the night, so that day and night no longer come at their appointed time, then my covenant with David my servant—and my covenant with the Levites who are priests ministering before me—can be broken and David will no longer have a descendant to reign on his throne. I will make the descendants of David my servant and the Levites who minister before me as countless as the stars of the sky and as measureless as the sand on the seashore.'" (Jer 33:15–22)

While the determinist interprets this as evidence of the unconditional covenant, when taken with the whole counsel of Scripture, we see that God is consistent in offering grace within the context of a conditional covenant. The determinist chooses a literalist interpretation of this text, although it speaks metaphorically of the coming of Jesus Christ.

The idea of the conditional covenant is not limited to the prophet Jeremiah. The prophet Ezekiel agrees:

"Therefore, son of man, say to your countrymen, 'The righteousness of the righteous man will not save him when he disobeys, and the wickedness of the wicked man will not cause him to fall when he turns from it. The righteous man, if he sins, will not be allowed to live because of his former righteousness.' If I tell the righteous man that he will surely live, but then he trusts in his righteousness and does evil, none of the righteous things he has done will be remembered; he will die for the evil he has done. And if I say to the wicked man, 'You will surely die,' but he then turns away from his sin and does what is just and right—if he gives back what he took in pledge for a loan, returns what he has stolen, follows the decrees that give life, and does no evil, he will surely live; he will not die. None of the sins he has committed will be remembered against him. He has done what is just and right; he will surely live." (Ezek 33:12–16)

Through the prophet Hosea, God says, "Because you have rejected knowledge, I also reject you as my priests; because you have ignored the law of your God, I also will ignore your children" (Hos 4:6). "My God will reject them because they have not obeyed him; they will be wanderers among the nations" (Hos 9:17). In the book of Zechariah, we read, "Then I took my staff called Favor and broke it, revoking the covenant I had made with all the nations. It was revoked on that day, and so the afflicted of the flock who were watching me knew it was the word of the LORD" (Zech 11:10–11). In order to support the idea of the unconditional covenant, the determinist must ignore all these scriptures.

Other scriptures appear to support determinism. Taken out of context, these may create an impression of indisputability. But taken in context and considered in the light of other scriptures, one can balance the interpretation.

Determinists insist that the covenant God made with David was unconditional and permanent. This drives the expectation that Israel will be restored in the last day. Often quoted is the covenant God made with David, "My love will never be taken away from him, as I took it away from Saul, whom I removed from before you. Your house and your kingdom will endure forever before me; your throne will be established forever" (2 Sam 7:15–16). Notice that this statement does not include the if-then language so common elsewhere in the Bible. What goes unmentioned by determinists is the very similar message given by God to Solomon:

"As for you, if you walk before me in integrity of heart and uprightness, as David your father did, and do all I command and observe my decrees and laws, I will establish your royal throne over Israel forever, as I promised David your father when I said, 'You shall never fail to have a man on the throne of Israel.'

> "But if you or your sons turn away from me and do not observe the commands and decrees I have given you and go off to serve other gods and worship them, then I will cut off Israel from the land I have given them and will reject this temple I have consecrated for my Name. Israel will then become a byword and an object of ridicule among all peoples. And though this temple is now imposing, all who pass by will be appalled and will scoff and say, 'Why has the LORD done such a thing to this land and to this temple?' People will answer, 'Because they have forsaken the LORD their God, who brought their fathers out of Egypt, and have embraced other gods, worshiping and serving them—that is why the LORD brought all this disaster on them.'" (1 Kings 9:4–9)

So much for an unconditional covenant! God *has* kept *all* of his promises to David and to Israel.

While we are considering whether the Davidic covenant is conditional or unconditional, we should look at Psalm 89. Remember that the Psalms are statements of worship by inspired writers rather than messages composed directly by God. Before we go further, let me invite you to read Psalm 89 itself. It is relevant to our discussion because it makes direct reference to the Davidic covenant. Clearly, the psalmist believes that God has made a permanent and irrevocable promise that a descendent of David will rule forever. However, the psalmist knows that there are consequences for disobedience. He implies that the people of God are being punished because they have failed to keep the covenant. Still, the psalmist remains convinced that God is faithful. He wonders aloud how long God will subject Israel to their just punishment (the exile) and begin to show mercy for the sake of his promises. Taken alone, this psalm seems to provide evidence of an unconditional covenant with Israel.

However, read Psalm 89 alongside the New Testament explanation that Jesus fulfills God's promise as the Son of David. The psalmist did not have this information, but we do. Paul goes to considerable length to explain that Jesus is the seed of Abraham (Gal 3:15–16). The genealogy that begins the gospel of Matthew calls Jesus "the son of David, the son of Abraham" (Matt 1:1). Paul began his letter to the Romans by describing Jesus as a son of David as well as the Son of God (1:3). Rather than waiting for Jesus to return for a millennial rule in the last day, the New Testament says that Jesus began fulfilling the Davidic covenant during his earthly ministry and is ruling on the throne of David today. (This present-day Kingdom theology is central to Church of God teaching.)

Instead of quoting the words of Jeremiah out of context ("This is what the LORD says: 'David will never fail to have a man to sit on the throne of the house of Israel'" [Jer 33:17]), we do well to recognize the context of this messianic prophecy. We have already looked at the thirty-third chapter of Jeremiah, which includes what seems to be an affirmation of unconditional covenant:

> The word of the LORD came to Jeremiah: "This is what the LORD says: 'If you can break my covenant with the day and my covenant with the night, so that day and night no longer come at their appointed time, then my covenant with David my servant—and my covenant with the Levites who are priests ministering before me—can be broken and David will no longer have a descendant to reign on his throne.'" (Jer 33:19–21)

While this seems to teach an unconditional covenant with Israel, we must take into consideration the verses that immediately precede it. From the perspective of the Christian era, we can see that God has not broken his covenant. The son of David has come and now rules on his throne.

The determinist insists that God has unfinished business for Israel because of promises he made through the prophets. But careful examination of these passages will show that they speak of the return from exile that happened before the first coming of Jesus.

> A remnant will return, a remnant of Jacob will return to the Mighty God. Though your people, O Israel, be like the sand by the sea, only a remnant will return. Destruction has been decreed, overwhelming and righteous. (Isa 10:21–22)

> "For a brief moment I abandoned you, but with deep compassion I will bring you back. In a surge of anger I hid my face from you for a moment, but with everlasting kindness I will have compassion on you," says the LORD your Redeemer. (Isa 54:7–8)

Following a time of exile, God restored Israel to the Promised Land. Some have observed that the worship of idols was never a problem among the Jews after the exile; they have been fiercely monotheistic. But when God sent the long-promised Messiah, many failed to receive him (John 1:11).

Perhaps the most difficult passage in the Bible to interpret related to the conditional covenant is Romans 9–11. For the determinist, this provides the irrefutable evidence that God's covenant is unconditional. Especially convincing are the statements "All Israel will be saved" (11:26) and "God's gifts and his call are irrevocable" (11:29). A careful exegesis of these passages would require more attention than can be given here. However, notice that the word *Israel* seems to refer not only to ethnic Jews but also to the body of Christ: "Not all who are descended from Israel are Israel" (9:6). Within the same context, Paul said, "There is no difference between Jew and Gentile" (10:12). God has no unfinished business with Israel. His covenant remains available to the Jew, as it has also been extended to the Gentile. The determinist creates a false hope that some persons can be saved apart from faith in Jesus Christ.

Calvinism is an imminently logical system, so it illustrates the limitations of deductive reasoning. While the premise that God is sovereign is sound, we can deduce from it doctrines that are not biblical. The

Church of God heritage has always held a more Arminian understanding of God's sovereignty. This understanding better fits the whole of Scripture studied inductively.

We believe that God offers salvation to anyone who will respond. Our freedom continues beyond the first encounter with Christ, however, so that we may terminate the relationship at any time if we so choose. Israel exercised this freedom poorly, leading to the loss of their earthly kingdom. God's new covenant extends to Jew and Gentile alike (Gal 3:28–29). Even while living within this covenant, we should not assume that everything which happens to us is a part of God's plan for our lives.

These teachings may be contrary to what is taught in evangelical[21] Christian circles, but they are biblical. Determinism has no place in Church of God thinking.

FOR FURTHER STUDY

Byrum, Russell R.. *Christian Theology*. Anderson, IN: Gospel Trumpet Company, 1925. See pp. 274–447.

Gray, Albert F. *Christian Theology*. Anderson, IN: Gospel Trumpet Company, 1944. See pp. 1:105–267; 2:45–74.

Stafford, Gilbert W. *Theology for Disciples*. Anderson, IN: Warner Press, 1996. See chap. 15, "God's Will in the Face of Evil and Suffering"; chap. 16, "Sin."

Oden, Thomas C. *Pastoral Theology: Essentials of Ministry*. San Francisco: HarperSanFranscisco, 1983. See chap. 15, "A Theodicy for Pastoral Practice."

QUESTIONS FOR DISCUSSION

1. How do you balance the doctrine of divine sovereignty with the doctrine of free will?

---

21. I am using *evangelical* in a restricted sense, as explained in the Introduction and Appendix B.

2. How do you resolve the tension between biblical texts that imply an unconditional covenant with those indicating that the covenant is conditional?

3. How do you respond to the teaching that God has not fulfilled all his promises to Israel, so Israel must play a pivotal role in the last days?

4. How do you answer the question, Why does a loving and all-powerful God allow suffering?

5. Why is determinism such a comforting belief system for some people? What does rejection of determinism do to Christian faith?

3.

Do You Have to Be Right or Get Left Behind?

JEN WIPED her eyes as the lights came up in the darkened auditorium. She had just seen graphic images she could never have imagined. The movie claimed to offer a dramatic portrayal of biblical prophecy. Crashing cars careened on freeways and airplanes plummeted from the sky as drivers and pilots were taken by the great rapture. A world leader survived a bloody head wound only to rise to greater levels of despotism. Armies, navies, air forces, and missile commands of Russia, China, and Arab countries were marshaled against the tiny country of Israel only to be mysteriously thwarted. Credit cards and social security numbers were utilized in a conspiracy to track every American citizen. Dollars, English pounds, Japanese yen and all other currencies were replaced by a single monetary unit as the economy of the world was brought under the control of a one-world government. Jen had grown up in a Christian family, had been active in her church youth group, and had read parts of the book of Revelation, but she had never seen or heard the things she saw in this movie. It all seemed too real. What should she believe?

We have seen a surge of interest in recent years in end-time theories. A significant portion of most Christian bookstores is devoted to Bible prophecy. On Christian radio and TV, prophecy experts prognosticate on the implications of current news stories in the light of biblical predictions. While evangelicals have long used film to communicate their end-time expectations, the recent Left Behind series has set record levels for film and video sales. All of this creates the impression that only one option exists for serious Christians when it comes to what we believe about Revelation and the second coming of Jesus Christ.

On the contrary, we find in the history of Christian thought at least four sets of options for interpreting Revelation and four sets of options for thinking about what will happen when Jesus comes again.

Discussions of the book of Revelation and similar books of the Bible involve *apocalyptic* interpretation.[1] Discussions of the last days and the return of Christ bring us into the area of theology known as *eschatology*.

The four choices in apocalyptic interpretation include the preterist interpretation (the symbols refer to actual events in the first century, such as the persecution under Emperor Nero), the historicist interpretation (the symbols predict events across the span of human history, most of which have been fulfilled), the futurist interpretation (the symbols predict events that will happen at the end of time and have not been fulfilled yet), and the idealist interpretation (the symbols are not predictions of historical events but a depiction of the ongoing battle between good and evil).

The four basic theological options in eschatology are dispensational premillennialism (found in the *Left Behind* series and many other modern evangelical sources), historic premillenialism (similar to dispensational premillennialism, except for its belief in a post-tribulation rapture), postmillenialism (a nearly extinct belief that the church will establish the Kingdom on earth and then Christ will return), and amillenialism (which rejects the idea of a physical, literal, historical rule of Christ on earth).

Premillennial dispensationalism (the theology behind the Left Behind stories) developed almost entirely in the past two hundred years. What many believe to be a classic Christian doctrine is a relatively new product of English and American culture. While elements of millennial beliefs emerged in previous church history, the dispensational system was largely unknown to the early church or to the Protestant

---

1. Unfortunately, many so-called experts do not seem to know the difference between prophecy and apocalyptic and label all of these scriptures as biblical prophecy. For an explanation of the difference, see Callen, *Faithful in the Meantime,* 48–52.

Reformation. Before 1800, premillennialism was taught only among fringe groups and heretics. The particular set of end-time beliefs so common among evangelicals today comes from the teachings of nineteenth-century writers like John Nelson Darby. At the beginning of the twentieth century, millennial theories were adopted by Fundamentalists in their revolt against liberalism. Dwight L. Moody and his Bible Prophecy Conferences spread this approach across the United States. Popular books on this topic included *Jesus Is Coming* by W. E. Blackstone. *The Scofield Study Bible* provided Christians with this new theory in the margins of Holy Scripture. In the early 1970s, the book *Late Great Planet Earth* by Hal Lindsey again fanned popular interest in dispensationalism. Lindsey and others identified the founding of the nation of Israel in 1948 as a key indicator that last-day events were unfolding. Many of the leading forces in evangelical[2] Christianity teach this approach to eschatology.

Millennial theories have always been foreign to the Church of God. A number of Church of God writers have refuted the claims of millennialism. During the early decades of the Church of God, interpretation of books like Revelation used a church-historical approach (which reads the symbols of apocalyptic literature as predicting the rise, apostasy, and restoration of the church). Some continue to prefer this approach to this day. However, for the last several decades, a growing number of Church of God scholars have chosen to take either a preterist or an idealist approach to apocalyptic literature. Whichever approach they use, Church of God writers have been consistent in affirming an amillennial eschatology. Amillennialists believe that the kingdom of God is a present-day reality among believers and that time will end when Jesus comes again. We find this present-day concept of the kingdom of God in several Church of God heritage songs.

> To Christ all power on earth is giv'n,
> > See now His mighty scepter's sway;

---

2. I am using *evangelical* in a restricted sense, as explained in the Introduction and Appendix B.

While others dream of an age to come,
He's reigning in our hearts today.[3]

Church of the Living God
We wait no future time;
But now on earth with joy we dwell
Within Thy courts sublime.[4]

F. G. Smith offered two leading books on apocalyptic interpretation and eschatology with *What the Bible Teaches* (1914) and *Revelation Explained* (1908). In these books, Smith follows the church-historical approach, which was adapted from what pioneer Church of God leader D. S. Warner found in the writings of Adventist writer Uriah Smith.[5] In discussing his rejection of millennial theories, F. G. Smith said, "There is not a thousand years after the last day."[6] Smith wrote at length, applying images from Revelation to key events in church history, culminating in the birth of the Church of God movement. Many Church of God ministers have followed the interpretation offered by F. G. Smith. Since 1930, however, a growing number of Church of God scholars (beginning with Otto F. Linn) have opted for other interpretations.

In his *Christian Theology*, R. R. Byrum dealt at length with the premillennial theory as it had developed in his day. He said,

This theory represents a distinct school of Scripture interpretation, which is highly revolutionary in nature. It affects some of the most important points in Christian doctrine. It is subversive of the whole aim and mission of the church. Its

---

3. Teasley, "We'll Crown Him Lord of All."

4. Teasley, "Church of the Living God."

5. Callen, *Faithful in the Meantime*, 42–43. The church-historical method taught by F. G. Smith was pioneered by D. S. Warner and H. M. Riggle. Recent writers who have carried on this tradition include Lillie McCutcheon and Richard Bradley. The development of church-historical interpretation from Warner to F.G. Smith is detailed in Strege, *I Saw the Church*, 95–112.

6. Smith, *What the Bible Teaches*, 339.

advocates become so obsessed with it that they believe they find references to it on almost every page of the Bible.[7]

In tracing the development of the theory, Byrum asserted that Jesus "neither established nor promised to establish such an earthly kingdom." He compared premillennial theories with Jewish apocalyptic expectations and said, "Though some eminent fathers held millenarianism, it was never generally accepted." In response to the claim that only liberals dispute premillennialism, Byrum said, "Before the rise of the modern school of criticism Christians generally rejected premillenarianism." In evaluating the claims of literal Bible interpretation made by dispensationalists, he found that they failed to understand the use of symbolic language in the Bible. Byrum criticized the way that premillenialists find predictions of the second coming throughout the Old Testament prophets, saying, "The prophets and Israel were not especially concerned about an event so remote as the second advent. A matter of far more immediate concern to them was the first advent of Christ." In refuting these claims, Byrum often made reference to Blackstone's well-known book.[8]

A. F. Gray also devoted a chapter to premillenialism in his *Christian Theology*. In discussing the single reference to a millennium in Revelation 20,[9] Gray said,

> A great amount is read into this scripture, which says nothing of a restored Jewish nation, or of any reign on earth, or of any connection with the return of Christ. It is not safe to place one's interpretation on so highly figurative a passage and then bend the plain statement of other scriptures to meet that interpretation. Such a practice is used freely in dealing with the Book of Revelation, and with this chapter in particular.[10]

---

7. Byrum, *Christian Theology*, 609.

8. Ibid., 609–20.

9. The only place that the millennium is mentioned in the entire Bible is in Revelation 20, which includes five occurrences of a "thousand years" (vv. 2–6).

10. Gray, *Christian Theology*, 2:213–14.

Gray criticized premillenialists for being inconsistent in their literal interpretation of biblical symbols. While dispensationalists pride themselves on "taking the Bible literally," some Bible passages are so clearly symbolic that even dispensationalists do not interpret them literally. Gray rejected the idea that the nation of Israel has continuing status as the people of God, saying, "All special rights of the Jews came to an end in Christ." He faulted premillenialists for twisting the meaning of prophetic passages beyond their intent so that the original message is destroyed.

> Many prophecies are warped out of their setting and given a modern meaning which cannot by any fair means be found in the prophecy or its context. Most all prophecy is applied to the present time in a way that makes it meaningless and valueless to all past ages.

In response to the idea of a postponed Kingdom (also known as the Great Parenthesis), Gray said,

> This idea is that Christ fully intended to set up his kingdom at his first coming, but the Jews rejected him, making it impossible for him to do so; therefore he postponed the setting up of the kingdom till his return. This explanation is offered in spite of the fact that the Jews sought by force to make him king and he refused to accept the throne.[11]

Gray presents the teaching of premillennial theory in much the same way as did Byrum, and in like manner rejected it as inadequate interpretation of Scripture.

H. M. Riggle, one of the first-generation preachers of the Church of God, gave a graphic refutation of the idea that Jesus failed in his mission to set up a physical kingdom in his life on earth.

---

11. Ibid., 2:209–18.

The vain, worldly expectation that the Messiah would establish a literal kingdom caused the Jews to reject him and his spiritual kingdom. They wanted only an earthly kingdom; hence rejected and crucified the Son of God. As soon as the church began to apostasize and to lose the glory of the spiritual kingdom, vain ambitions awakened the old Jewish desire for a literal kingdom. And so it has come to pass that at this time of dead formality we have a multitude of men teaching the same error and false hope that crucified Christ nearly nineteen hundred years ago; namely, a literal kingdom of Christ.[12]

In similar manner, current Church of God thinkers have seen premillennial hopes having more in common with misguided Jewish expectations than with God's plan.

Rather than refute the claims of premillennialism directly, Gilbert W. Stafford has chosen to express more positively a biblical eschatology. In his *Theology of Disciples,* Stafford gives a panoramic survey of biblical teaching about the Kingdom.[13] In a presentation at the 2004 Church of God North American Convention, Stafford summarized a New Testament eschatology by describing what can be expected at the end of time. In that presentation, Stafford addressed several specific questions that arise from the teachings of premillennialists. In his view, the rapture described in 1 Thessalonians 4:17 ushers in an eternity with the Lord. Stafford identifies the great tribulation as "the ongoing turmoil surrounding the destruction of the temple in AD 70." Stafford describes the millennium as "the indefinite period of time between the first and second coming of our Lord." He believes the rebuilding of the temple refers to the church. Of the claim that the birth of Israel in 1948 was a fulfillment of biblical prophecy, Stafford says, "The modern state of Israel is a secular state, not the people of God spoken of in Scripture. As Paul says in Romans 2:29, 'A person is a Jew who is one inwardly,

---

12. Riggle, *Christ's Kingdom and Reign* , 51.
13. Stafford, *Theology for Disciples*, 73–99.

and real circumcision is a matter of the heart—it is spiritual and not literal.' (See also Luke 3:7–9; John 8:31–59; Ephesians 3:1–6.)"[14]

Amillennial eschatology has been the norm throughout the history of the Church of God. Yet some Church of God people today are adopting dispensationalism because of the pervasive influence of books, movies, and preachers outside the movement. Church of God interpretation shows little interest in the great tribulation, the rapture, Armageddon, the Beast, the number 666, and all the other curious symbols that so fascinate millennialists.[15] Over against the complex scenarios offered by premillennialists, the Church of God has always believed that we are now experiencing the Kingdom as we have since its establishment in the first century, and we await the return of Christ when he will bring all time to an end and gather us into glory.

As mentioned earlier, for the first fifty years of the movement, the primary view of apocalyptic in the Church of God was the historicist (or church-historical) interpretation. From D. S. Warner to H. M. Riggle to F. G. Smith, our books interpreted the book of Revelation as showing that the Church of God was predicted by the Bible as part of God's plan for the "Evening Light." Whereas the dispensationalist sees future political leaders of the great tribulation in the images of Revelation, those who follow the church-historical approach see religious leaders and groups from both the past and present. For writers like F. G. Smith, the Beast and the False Prophet became the Roman Catholic Church and Protestantism. (Most current Church of God scholars challenge this interpretation.)

Since the 1930s, Church of God thinking has progressively moved to the preterist and/or idealist interpretation. There are still some people in the Church of God who hold to the historicist view. These tend to center around the periodical *Reformation Witness* and the Winchester Pastor's Fellowship. In the 1960s, Lillie McCutcheon wrote *The Symbols Speak,* which carried the historicist approach into the cold war.

---

14. Stafford, "Eschatology."

15. Callen notes that this lack of preoccupation with end-time events is common to Wesleyan-Holiness people (Callen, *Faithful in the Meantime*, 55.).

Richard W. Bradley is the latest Church of God author to take a historicist approach.

These discussions are not just a matter of understanding future mysteries. This involves the vital work of hermeneutics (how to interpret Scripture). I have observed poor interpretation, including prooftexting, in the writing of many dispensationalists. I find a lot in common between the errors of futurists and historicists. Both twist Scripture mercilessly to fit their preconceived notions. While fanciful images abound in the book of Revelation, we must be sober in interpreting their meaning. Revelation was written to inspire a church under persecution. Those who find Saddam Hussein and nuclear missiles there are surely missing the point. Those who search for predictive calendars are also surely missing the point of apocalyptic literature. Those who adopt a historicist approach seem awfully narcissistic. (Do we really think the book of Revelation is all about us?) The French Revolution may have been a major event from the perspective of 1908 when F. G. Smith wrote *Revelation Explained*, but it seems like ancient history to people today. Where Church of God historicists see the story climaxing in 1880, they learned this method of interpretation from Uriah Smith (an adventist), who had worked the numbers to climax in 1843. That was when many American adventists stood on hillsides dressed in white, awaiting the return of Christ.

Church of God writers have given a great deal of attention to the theme of the kingdom of God. What they have in mind is not an earthly kingdom to be established at Christ's second coming, but a present-day reality established by Jesus in his first advent. This emphasis on the kingdom has been shared by all Church of God writers, whether or not they agree on their interpretation of apocalyptic literature. The lyrics of a song recorded by Sandi Patty describe well the sentiment of Church of God people about the kingdom of God and the misrepresentations made by many premillenialists.

> While men search for crowns and thrones,
> He walked with crowds—alone,
> Planting a seed in you and me...

And some of them looked for Him,

Sad that it had to end,

But some dared to look within and see!

The kingdom of God, a kingdom that would never end...

The living unshakeable kingdom of God.

Still some of us look for him,

Sad that it has to end

Do we dare to look within and see

The kingdom of God, a kingdom that would never end...

The living unshakeable kingdom of God.[16]

The Church of God holds a very different vision of the future than do most evangelicals. While evangelicals generally rally around the teachings of dispensational premillennialism with its pretribulation rapture, the Church of God subscribes to an amillennial eschatology. The Church of God is less unified in its interpretation of Revelation and other books of apocalyptic literature such as Daniel. Many continue to hold to the early church-historical interpretation, which reads Revelation as a prophetic timetable of church history leading to the end of time. However, a growing consensus of Church of God ministers see the church-historical interpretation as incorrect and have adopted either a preterist or idealist interpretation. They see the book of Revelation as a portrayal of first-century issues or as a timeless depiction of the battle between good and evil. In the face of a popular wave of interest in the Left Behind series, Church of God people should hold fast to a sound interpretation of apocalyptic Scripture as we await the return of our Lord.

---

16. "Unshakeable Kingdom," lyrics by Gloria Gaither, music by William J. Gaither and Michael W. Smith.

Callen, Barry L. *Faithful in the Meantime: A Biblical View of Final Things and Present Responsibilities.* Nappanee, IN: Evangel Publishing House, 1997.

Strong, Marie. *A Common Sense Approach to the Book of Revelation.* Edited by Sharon Clark Pearson. Anderson, IN: Warner Press, 1996.

Stafford, Gilbert W. "Eschatology." Paper, Doctrinal Dialogue, North American Conference of the Church of God, Anderson, IN, June 30, 2004. http://www.anderson.edu/ccl/eschatology.pdf.

Strege, Merle. *I Saw the Church.* Anderson, IN: Warner Press, 2002. See pp. 95–112.

Gaulke, Max. *May Thy Kingdom Come—Now.* Anderson, IN: Warner Press, 1959.

Byrum, Russell R. *Christian Theology.* Anderson, IN: Gospel Trumpet Company, 1925. See part 7, "Last Things, or Eschatology."

Gray, Albert F. *Christian Theology.* Anderson, IN: Gospel Trumpet Company, 1944. See pp. 2:195–265.

Stafford, Gilbert W. *Theology for Disciples.* Anderson, IN: Warner Press, 1996. See pp. 93–99.

Smith, Frederick G. *Revelation Explained.* Anderson, IN: Gospel Trumpet Company, 1908.

Riggle, Herbert M. *Christ's Kingdom and Reign.* Anderson, IN: Gospel Trumpet Co., 1918

Cox, William E. *Amillennialism TODAY.* Philipsburg, NJ: Presbyterian and Reformed Publishing, 1966.

Peterson, Eugene H. *Reversed Thunder.* San Francisco: HarperSanFrancisco, 1988.

Questions for Discussion

1. Compare and contrast the four approaches to eschatology.
   - Historic Premillennialism
   - Dispensational Premillennialism

- Postmillennialism
- Amillennialism

2. Compare and contrast the four approaches to interpretation of apocalyptic literature.
   - Preterist
   - Futurist
   - Historicist
   - Idealist

3. What difference does it make in the life of a Christian if the kingdom of God is present or future?

4. What difference does it make if the church-historicists are right, and the Church of God movement is predicted in Revelation?

5. Some have suggested that the Church of God movement has lost its sense of mission since abandoning the church-historical interpretation of Bible prophecy. Do you agree?

6. How should your congregation respond to the popularity of the Left Behind series?

4.

Might the Best Man for Your Church Be a Woman?

RACHEL WAS in the first week of college. She had come with high hopes of serving the Lord in ministry. This had been her passion for two years since hearing the call from God during youth camp after her sophomore year of high school. She had chosen this school because her pastor had graduated from there and her church included the college in their budget. Now she was far from home and building a new circle of friends. Friday night, Rachel joined in a conversation at the student center with a half dozen other students. Most of these students were also freshmen. The conversation turned to, "What is your major?"

Rachel shared that she had come to college to study Bible and prepare for service as a pastor. This triggered a debate as three young men challenged her dream. "Don't you know that God only calls men to be pastors?" one of them asked. Rachel was aware that most ministers were men, but she knew two women pastors whose ministry had shaped her life profoundly. The ferocity of this debate left her traumatized. As she sat alone in her dorm room that night, Rachel was emotionally shaken. She was literally shaking as she wept in the darkness. *What have you gotten me into?* she asked the Lord.

While some evangelical[1] Christians are open to women in ministry, many insist that it is a violation of God's will for a woman to serve as a pastor. Anyone open to the idea is labeled a "liberal" along with mainline denominations like the Episcopal Church that have recently opened the doors to women for ordination. Some evangelical groups

---

1. I am using *evangelical* in a restricted sense, as explained in the Introduction and Appendix B.

are openly asserting that only men are called by God to be pastors. The Church of God, on the other hand, has always understood that God calls women as well as men to ministry of various types.

This recognition of the call of God on the lives of women was remarkable in the first fifty years of the Church of God.

> The pioneers of the Church of God such as D. S. Warner, considered women equal to men. Women were a part of the evangelizing teams. They served as exhorters and counselors. Somewhat later they also served as evangelists and pastors. They have been highly successful too.[2]

Among Warner's famous team of traveling evangelists (known then as "flying messengers") were three women—Nannie Kigar, Frankie Miller, and "Mother" Sarah Smith. Sarah Smith testified, "I was filled with power and the Holy Ghost and such boldness. All that man-fearing spirit was taken away, and my heart was overflowing with perfect love that was so unspeakable and full of glory."[3] In *What the Bible Teaches*, F. G. Smith said, "Christianity is the only religion in the world that recognizes men and women as equals."[4] Smith further declared, "The work of God needs men and women who are consecrated to evangelize the world."[5] C. W. Naylor wrote in the *Gospel Trumpet*,

> There are today multitudes of souls who have been brought to Christ through the ministry of faithful, Spirit-anointed women. To condemn their work in such a capacity is to condemn the God whose blessing is upon their labors and who saves souls and who hears them. Beware lest you fight against God.[6]

---

2. Koglin, "The Status of Women in the Church," 17–18.
3. Susie Stanley, "Women Evangelists," 39.
4. Smith, *What the Bible Teaches*, 177.
5. Ibid, 183.
6. Naylor, "Questions Answered," 262.

C. E. Brown spoke further to the issue in the *Gospel Trumpet*:

> As a matter of fact, the prevalence of women preachers is
> a fair measure of the spirituality of a church, a country, or
> an age. As the church grows more apostolic and more deep-
> ly spiritual, women preachers and workers abound in the
> church; as it grows more worldly and cold, the ministry of
> women is despised and gradually ceases altogether.[7]

> Probably one of the greatest sources of the weakness of the
> modern church is that it has refused women the opportunity
> for distinguished service within its ranks. By thus closing the
> door in the face of millions of its most talented and conse-
> crated workers it has diverted their strength into hundreds
> of other social agencies and thus robbed itself of an incalcu-
> lable influence in the modern world.[8]

Since 1940, the Church of God has failed to live up to this heritage
as the number of women called to serve as pastors has fallen dramatically. Merle Strege notes that this trend began about the time C. E.
Brown became editor of the *Gospel Trumpet*.[9] This is ironic as Brown
was among our early leaders who championed the cause of women
in ministry. Several have documented that the high point for women
serving as Church of God pastors was in 1925, when more than 30
percent of our pastors were women. In the decades that followed, the
percentage of women serving as pastors of local churches has fallen to
below 5 percent.[10] Juanita Evans Leonard tracks the statistical decline
of women in Church of God ministry in the twentieth century.[11] Strege

---

7. Brown, "Women as Preachers," 5.

8. Ibid., 13.

9. Strege, *I Saw the Church*, 220.

10. Leonard, "Women, Change, and the Church," 152, 157; Strege, *I Saw the Church*,
324.

11. Leonard, "Women, Change, and the Church," 152–64.

chronicles the contributions of several exceptional women, including Jennie Carpenter Ruttie, Elsie Egermeier, Nora Hunter, Marie Strong, Lillie McCutcheon, and Cheryl J. Sanders.[12] Several students of our history have observed that Church of God people have been influenced by certain evangelical thinking to betray our heritage in this regard.

A "fundamentalist leavening" also accounts for the anti-woman mentality, particularly in this generation. Churches and individuals who oppose women in ministry have promoted their opinions aggressively through the print medium and on television Insisting on their literal interpretation of scripture, they accuse other churches that ordain women of being influenced by the current revival of the women's movement.[13]

David Markle, pastor at Park Place Church of God in Anderson, Indiana, and my predecessor as professor at Warner Pacific College, has been quoted as saying, "Perhaps the reason we struggle to find enough pastors to fill all our pulpits is that we turn our backs on half of the people whom God has lifted up for ministry!"

Leaders in the Church of God have called the movement to again honor the call that God places on women. The General Assembly of the Church of God passed a resolution in June 1974 including this statement: "RESOLVED, that more women be given opportunity and consideration for positions of leadership in the total program of the Church of God, locally, statewide, and nationally."[14] In an edition of *Vital Christianity* devoted to the subject of women in ministry, Editor Arlo Newell said, *"For men only* is neither scriptural nor spiritual in the Christian community."[15] In his doctoral dissertation, Randal Huber echoes the old teachings of F. G. Smith by saying, "Leadership in the church is based upon spiritual gifts, not upon sex."[16] Huber goes on to

---

12. Strege, *I Saw the Church*, 323–30.
13. Susie Stanley, "Women Evangelists," 178.
14. Callen, *Following the Light*, 247–48.
15. Newell, "For Men Only?" 12–13.
16. Huber, *Called*, 21.

examine the biblical texts most often used to argue that God does not call women to ministry. He argues that a paradigm shift in pastoral ministry is needed today. Among the topics discussed by Huber are creation and the fall; leadership in the Old Testament; Jesus and women; Paul's teaching on women; stay-at-home moms; stereotypes versus reality; a modern feminist thing; and how to bring change.[17]

Rather than accepting the infrequency of women in ministry as evidence of the will of God, Huber argues, "Male dominance and female subjugation are the result of sin."[18] "Because of the curse of sin, men have dominated virtually everywhere. God has, however, always called women to be preachers or leaders. Sinful human cultures do not encourage women to preach or lead. Sinful human cultures minimize what women have to say, even when they speak for God...To argue that male headship means that the man is the woman's leader is to distort God's original intent in marriage."[19] In response to the allegations that godless feminism is the motive behind the drive to ordain women, Huber says, "Advancing women in ministry is not a feminist issue; it's a biblical issue."[20] Pastor Ronald J. Fowler stated it even more forcefully: "This is not a feminist issue, this is a SIN issue."[21] All this is in keeping with the lyric of our old hymn, "All we are equal in His sight when we obey His Word."[22]

Since those who argue against women in ministry base their position on biblical texts, we must consider what the Bible teaches on this subject. Key texts used to teach that God does not call women to ministry are 1 Timothy 2:11–15 and 1 Corinthians 14:33–34. These verses clearly instruct women to keep silent in church. "Women should remain silent in the churches. They are not allowed to speak, but must be in submission, as the Law says" (1 Cor 14:34). Those who point to

---

17. Ibid., 15–21; 32–38, 40–48, 50–64, 66–76, 79–94, 96–101, 108, 112.

18. Ibid., 34.

19. Ibid., 38.

20. Ibid., 98.

21. Ron Fowler, quoted in Clergy Task Force, *Go Preach My Gospel.*

22. Naylor, "The Church's Jubilee."

this verse as reason to exclude women from pastoral ministry ignore the fact that Paul wrote in the same letter, "And every woman who prays or prophesies with her head uncovered dishonors her head—it is just as though her head were shaved" (1 Cor 11:5). Whatever interpretation we might draw from Paul's words, we must recognize that he had no objection to women praying or prophesying in church.[23] If we are to adopt a literal interpretation of this verse, then every church must require that every woman wear a head covering.

> A woman should learn in quietness and full submission. I do not permit a woman to teach or to have authority over a man; she must be silent. For Adam was formed first, then Eve. And Adam was not the one deceived; it was the woman who was deceived and became a sinner. But women will be saved through childbearing—if they continue in faith, love and holiness with propriety. (1 Tim 2:11–15)

If a literal interpretation is correct, then the Christian role for women is to keep getting pregnant! Those who refrain from drawing this conclusion but say that women can only teach other women or children are practicing inconsistent biblical interpretation. F. G. Smith recognized the fact that this verse was being interpreted in this way, saying, "It is evident that 1 Timothy 2:11–15 does not cover the subject of women's official position in the church as set forth in the other scriptures; for such an application would involve a contradiction between texts. It applies, instead, to the proper relationship of the woman with her own husband."[24]

Those who accept the idea that God calls women to ministry tend to cite Galatians 3:28 as the cornerstone text on the matter: "There is neither Jew nor Greek, slave nor free, male nor female, for you are all one in Christ Jesus" (Gal 3:28). This anthem of inclusion is the basis of the principle of Christian unity, as opposed to division and separatism.

---

23. John E. Stanley, "New Testament Arguments,." 54; Huber, *Called,* 57–58.

24. Smith, *What the Bible Teaches,* 181; see also Huber and Stanley, *Reclaiming the Wesleyan/Holiness Heritage;* see also Huber, *Called,* 58–64.

However, some evangelicals argue that this verse refers only to salvation and not to church leadership and polity.

The fact that Jesus called only men to be among the Twelve is proffered as the model for church leadership. In response, Sharon Pearson reminds us that no Gentile was chosen for this group, either.[25] To be consistent on this matter, evangelicals should only recognize Jewish men as their pastors. We should beware of such selective hermeneutic. While all of those named among the Twelve were men, women were among the disciples of Jesus. In fact, "Women supported Jesus and his disciples financially."[26] The very fact that Jesus spoke with women and included them in his circle of friends was revolutionary in a culture that practiced gender segregation, much like that practiced by fundamentalist Muslims today. The belief that women are unqualified to be pastors can blind many Christians to what the Scriptures actually report. The gospel of Luke, in particular, displays the unprecedented interest Jesus had in working with women. "Last at the cross, and earliest at the grave (or tomb)" was a line often used in the Church of God to speak of the New Testament record of women in ministry.[27]

To defend the idea that only men should be pastors, some refer to the "headship" teaching of Ephesians 5. This argument has several flaws. The passage is not speaking of ministry qualifications but of the marriage relationship: "For the husband is the head of the wife as Christ is the head of the church, his body, of which he is the Savior" (Eph 5:23). To use a text that discusses relations between a husband and wife to deny women authority in the Church constitutes a misuse of Scripture.[28] Even if we concede the idea that the husband is head of the wife (i.e., that the husband is in some sense dominant over the wife), this has no relevance to relationships in the church. Arguing that this verse gives every man authority over every woman in the church stretches the application far beyond the original intent. Quoting these words to claim

---

25 Pearson, "Biblical Precedents," 17.

26. Ibid., 15; see Luke 8:1–3.

27. Susie Stanley, "Women Evangelists," 40.

28. Pearson, "Biblical Precedents," 33.

that men are superior to women abuses the concept of headship.[29] As Huber says it, "The notion that 'head' should be understood as 'superior' or 'leader' does not come from the Bible. It is foreign to the Greek. It finds its sources in some patristic fathers, John Calvin, and common usage of the English language"[30] Here we find a classic example of taking a verse out of context to make it say something foreign to the Bible. This passage begins with, "Submit to one another out of reverence for Christ" (Eph 5:21). Submission is a mutual obligation, both in marriage and in the Church. This thesis verse is easily overlooked because many English translations separate it from the twenty-third verse, as though it is the last statement of the previous passage.

In Colossians, we find a somewhat parallel passage which includes the command, "Wives, submit to your husbands, as is fitting in the Lord" (Col 3:18). Sharon Pearson notes that Paul was taking common expectations of culture and joining them with uncommon imperatives from God in a poetic stream. The poetic structure of the Colossians text indicates that we should not interpret the first half of each couplet as a command from the Lord; rather, the divine command is always given in the second statement.[31] Pearson offers a refreshingly different approach than that often taken by evangelicals.

Huber observes, "A patriarchal cultural bias prevents some from seeing how God used women in the Bible."[32] A commonly mentioned example is Paul's reference to Phoebe in Romans 16:11. The apostle identifies Phoebe with a Greek word from which we get the English word *deacon*. Many modern translations render this word as *servant*, though elsewhere they render the same word as *minister*. This is an apparent example of theological bias in translation.

Another overlooked reference is Paul's mention of an apostle named Junia in Romans 16:7. The effort to hide this becomes almost

---

29. Sharon Clark Pearson offers a plain explanation of the meaning of "head" (*kephale*).

30. Huber, *Called*, 74.

31. Pearson, "Biblical Precedents," 24.

32. Huber, "Women Leaders," 33.

conspiratorial, as most English-language translators add the letter *s* to change this from a female name to a male name. Suggests Huber, "To concede that Junia was an apostle violates centuries of teaching that prohibited women from being leaders."[33] Women preachers in the Church of God often referred to Psalm 68:11 as translated by Adam Clark, "Of the female preachers there was great host."[34] Recognizing that the Bible does have verses that are difficult to interpret, Sharon Pearson says, "There is a tension between the eschatological vision (end times) of the prophet Joel as quoted on the day of Pentecost (Acts) and statements based upon propriety and convention."[35]

Some find it difficult to consider that God may call women to ministry because long-standing church tradition so strongly argues for male dominance.[36] It cannot be denied that most of the church over the last two thousand years has reserved ordination for men only. While we are wise to consider the voice of tradition, there are times when godly Bible students must protest traditional interpretations. To deny this is to preclude the Protestant Reformation and the hermeneutical tradition of the Church of God itself. It appears to me that strong political pressure is exerted in evangelical churches to silence those whose study of the Bible might cause them to question traditional practice. Disciplinary action may result in termination from ministry for those who go against the grain on this dogma.

In affirming the role of women in ministry, the Church of God movement has acted in concert with the Holiness Movement where it began. Bryan Wilson observes, "The holiness movement in its varied forms brought women to the fore, perhaps more than any previous development in Christianity."[37] The greater occurrence of women in ministry is rooted in the Wesleyan quadrilateral, John Wesley's four-

---

33. Ibid., 34, 54.

34. Susie Stanley, "Women Evangelists," 40.

35. Pearson, "Biblical Precedents," 14.

36. I am thinking here of the importance of tradition in the Wesleyan quadrilateral as discussed below.

37. Susie Stanley, "Women Evangelists," 36.

fold test of any Christian practice (Scripture / tradition / reason / experience). For example, it is hard to deny that God has called women into ministry when we experience women as such effective preachers and pastors. "Women's experiences of God's call have been consistent enough to become a valuable tradition, even a distinctive, of the Wesleyan/Holiness movement," says John Stanley.[38]

The debate about women in ministry has created an interesting array of allies and opponents. The Church of God heritage clearly differs from the common view among evangelicals when it comes to this issue. Modern evangelicals are allied with the Roman Catholic Church and the Mormons (Church of Jesus Christ, Latter Day Saints) in this conviction. On the other hand, the Church of God finds common cause with many liberal mainstream Protestants and Pentecostals in the conviction that God calls women *and* men to ministry. How odd that we find such bedfellows. Evangelicals have plenty of other reasons to differ with Catholics and Mormons over theology and biblical interpretation, while the Church of God has significant differences with both liberal mainstream Protestantism and Pentecostalism. But when it comes to women being called to ministry, our battle lines divide the theological landscape quite differently.

For the last several years, I have been privileged to teach ministry courses at a Church of God college. A growing number of my students are women. Many of these women have reported harshly negative experiences in ministry classes at other colleges. It would be an exaggeration to say that every woman in my classes is more gifted than the men. I find variety in the type and depth of giftedness among women, just as there is among men. However, the sad thing is that these women often find themselves "hitting the wall" when they complete their ministerial studies and try to find their first pastoral assignment. A number of Church of God congregations are unwilling to take them seriously. We must return to our heritage and practice what we have always preached.

---

38. John Stanley, "New Testament Arguments," 54.

I believe that we in the Church of God hold a secret weapon for reaching a culture that is tired of discrimination on the basis of gender. If we can spread the word that we have always believed that God calls both women and men to ministry, I imagine that we could find a ready response among the unchurched in our communities. This can start with you. There is probably a gifted woman preacher near you. Invite her to preach at your church. When your church is seeking a pastor, see if God might have just the woman for you.

Most modern evangelicals will probably continue to discriminate against women who sense a call from God to ministry. This does not have to be so in the Church of God movement. We can offer women the opportunity to obey God in whatever calling he ordains for their lives.

For Further Study

Huber, Randal. *Called, Equipped & No Place to Go: Women Pastors and the Church.* Anderson, IN: Warner Press, 2003.

Huber, Randy, and John Stanley. *Reclaiming the Wesleyan/Holiness Heritage of Women Clergy: Sermons, a Case Study and Resources.* Grantham, PA: Wesleyan/Holiness Women Clergy, 1999.

Leonard, Juanita Evans, ed. *Called to Minister Empowered to Serve.* Anderson, IN: Warner Press, 1989.

Oden, Thomas C. *Pastoral Theology: Essentials of Ministry.* San Francisco: HarperSanFranscisco, 1983. See chap. 4, "Women in the Pastoral Office."

Clergy Task Force. *Go Preach My Gospel: Women in Ministry.* Second Editon. VHS. Anderson, IN: Church of God Ministries, 2004.

Grady, J. Lee. *10 Lies the Church Tells Women: How the Bible Has Been Misused to Keep Women in Spiritual Bondage.* Lake Mary, Fla.: Creation House, 2000.

1. How does the Wesleyan quadrilateral inform your views of whether women should be ordained for ministry?

2. Have you known any women pastors? How does your observation of them inform your view on the ordination of women?

3. How do you respond to the fact that most of church tradition has held that women cannot be ordained to ministry?

4. How do you interpret these verses as they apply to the issue of women in ministry?
   - 1 Timothy 2:11–15
   - 1 Corinthians 14:33–34
   - 1 Corinthians 11:5

5. Brainstorm ways the Church of God can practice what it preaches concerning women in ministry.

5.

Is a Call All It Takes to Be a Pastor?

"**Y**OU YOUNG Turks think schooling is so important! I have been a minister of the gospel for fifty-three years. I have never cluttered my mind with the thoughts of men! All I need is the Word of God and the Holy Spirit. That's what the Church of God has always stood for! If God has not called you, then it doesn't matter how many degrees you have or if some credentials committee has voted on you! Give me one preacher who is called of God over a dozen cemetery graduates!" This exchange took place in the hallway during a pastor's meeting. Jeff, a college student preparing for ministry, had been speaking with Harry, a middle-aged pastor he viewed a mentor, about his latest studies. One of the older pastors overheard the conversation and joined in with this commentary.

Some fail to see any value in ministerial preparation and credentialing. For such persons, the only thing that matters is divine calling. The principle is, if God has called an individual to preach, then no one should interfere. While other chapters in this book address issues raised by modern evangelicals,[1] this chapter addresses an issue that has arisen from with our Church of God heritage. Some evangelicals deny the value of formal ministerial preparation and ordination, but there have always been persons in the Church of God who have questioned the legitimacy of schools for ministry or of credentialing committees.

While a divine calling is a prerequisite to effective ministry, there remains a need for ministerial preparation. Training has value in any field. Arguing that God's calling is more important than formal educa-

---

1. I am using *evangelical* in a restricted sense, as explained in the Introduction and Appendix B.

tion implies that the two should be separated. Formal academic work in a college and/or seminary offers a time-tested procedure for preparing individuals for pastoral ministry. The fact that some notable ministers were not blessed with such opportunities does not invalidate education.

The church as the body of Christ bears a responsibility to certify the call of God on individuals to serve in ministry. As Gilbert W. Stafford says,

> The ministries of the church's offices, by their very nature, require that special attention be given both to preparation for them and the church's ordination procedures regarding them. While the New Testament gives no outline for the preparation of its ministerial officers, it is clear that charismatic endowment is not enough.[2]

> Adequate preparation for the ordained ministry requires charismatic endowment, emotional and spiritual maturity, a divine call, and comprehensive studies—all four. Whenever the church lays hands of ordination on a person whose preparation is lacking in *any one* of these four components, it does so at its own great peril.[3]

One could cite exceptions in the lives of great pastors, both present and past. However, the apostle Paul was not one of them. The great apostle had a superior education before he came to Christ. Saul had rabbinical training under Gamaliel, one of the most highly respected rabbis (professors) of the day (Acts 22:3). Paul's academic preparation served him well in his theological analysis, preaching, the administration of his ministry, and the writing of his letters. Some seem to believe that Saul went directly from his encounter with Jesus on the Damascus trail to his three missionary journeys. The biblical record indicates

---

2. Stafford, *Theology for Disciples*, 197–98.
3. Ibid., 199.

otherwise. The book of Acts describes Saul carrying out ministry immediately in Damascus until threats to his life required that he relocate to Tarsus. Paul's own letter to the Galatians tells of a three-year time of study and reflection in Arabia after he was called to preach the gospel (Gal 1:11–18). Surely, this was a time when he had to rethink everything he had ever learned from the great rabbi in the light of his personal encounter with the risen Christ.[4] He then received a full year of on-the-job-training under the mentoring of Barnabas (Acts 11:25–26). He worked as the protégé of Barnabas at the church in Antioch until the two of them were sent out on a missions trip by the leadership of that church (Acts 13:1–3). The first great missionary journey can be viewed as the final phase of his education under Barnabas. During this trip, Saul (or Paul) grew in stature so that he began to eclipse his mentor. After they returned from that trip, they began to plan a second trip. Because of their difference of opinion over whether to take a younger protégé, these two men parted company and Paul ventured forth as an established missionary in his own right (Acts 15 36–40). By this time, Paul was a mature preacher with years of formal education and practical experience under the guidance of Barnabas and other leaders of the church. Paul stands as a great example of what can happen with proper training and supervision.

Within the heritage of the Church of God we find a paradox concerning ministerial education. Since the very beginning, leaders in the Church of God have often held ministerial education in low regard. Others established Bible colleges and liberal-arts colleges with a vision for formal ministerial education. To this day, we have both types of people in the Church of God: some who devote their lives to providing formal education for ministers and some who deny the value of formal education, casting aspersions on those who pursue academic disciplines.

---

4. Of course, the context of this is Paul's assertion that his apostolic authority came directly from God, arguing that he did not meet with Peter and the others until after this three-year period. I see no conflict between this and the conjecture of what he must have been doing with that time alone.

In the early days of the Church of God, there was almost no organization of the church. The idea was to let the Holy Spirit lead without the encumbrances of "man-rule." Over the years, we learned that we had to have certain ways of regulating ministry. A number of persons presented themselves as Church of God missionaries and asked people for financial support. A Missionary Committee began in 1909 to determine who should serve in what field and to avoid duplication of effort.[5] This group later developed into the Missions Board and today's Global Missions of Church of God Ministries, Inc.

On the home front, a similar need motivated the publication of the annual *Yearbook of the Church of God*. Ever since 1917, the Church of God has maintained this list of people authorized to represent the Church of God as ordained pastors. A key development in the process of ordination and credentialing was the publication of *Our Ministerial Letter* from 1912 to 1917. This was a more advanced leadership resource than the *Gospel Trumpet*. In August 1917, a plan for ministerial preparation was published by a group of key leaders.[6]

The authority to grant ministerial credentials is generally held by area (usually state) assemblies. Credentials committees in each assembly work to determine who is qualified for ordination. These committees are staffed with ordained pastors who interview prospective ministers, prescribe appropriate preparation, and provide mentoring. Because of differences in procedure between various assemblies, a common process has been developed and published in a *Credentials Manual*. By working in coordination with other credentials committees, state assemblies seek to protect the church from unscrupulous persons who try to move from one area to another without being held accountable for their actions. (Unfortunately, resistance to such coordination can still allow persons to bring harm to the Church of God.)

However, few of our state assemblies require an academic degree to be ordained for ministry. Those who argue that a college education

---

5. Strege, *I Saw the Church*, 82–27.

6. Callen, *Preparing for Service*, 20–21. See also Smith, *Quest for Holiness*, 148; and Strege, *I Saw the Church*, 85.

should not be required for service in ministry can find precedent to the beginning of the Church of God reformation movement. Barry L. Callen reports:

> The pioneers of this movement, therefore, were heavily experience-oriented (in common with many conservative Christians of the time) and also were quite anti-institutional in general outlook. They were disgusted with denominational rivalries and were less than impressed with the tendency of denominations to found colleges as part of that competitive process. The emphasis on experience and away from institutions, plus the general tenor of the times, led to considerable caution about the appropriateness of actually establishing "Church of God" institutions for the purpose of fostering the life of the mind. [7]

Quite understandably, education got off to a very slow start in the Church of God.

D. S. Warner claimed in the *Gospel Trumpet* that "the only credentials required for ministry were 'to be filled with the Holy Spirit and have a reasonable knowledge of the English language.'"[8] Warner rejected formal education as a tool of Catholicism and denominationalism, "as to men prescribing a course of study as a condition of preaching the Gospel, that is the vilest form of popery."[9] Warner further wrote, "Colleges are necessary to prepare men for the work of the devil and the business of the world...They are but the devil's playhouses."[10]

Warner was writing *The Cleansing of the Sanctuary* at the time of his death in 1895 and H. M. Riggle completed the book. There, we find another dismissal of the role of colleges: "All sects have their peculiar mark or doctrine with which they mark their subjects. They have erect-

---

7. Callen, *Preparing for Service*, 9–10.

8. Ibid., 13.

9. *Gospel Trumpet*, Dec. 1, 1883, cited in Callen, *Preparing for Service*, 14.

10. *Gospel Trumpet*, Oct. 15, 1884, cited by Callen, *Preparing for Service*, 13.

ed preacher factories for the express purpose of marking their ministers with their particular mark."[11]

A few years later, D. Otis Teasley wrote a blistering critique of ministerial schools in the *Gospel Trumpet:*

> Having recently seen some sad effects of human effort to train men and women for the ministry, I feel led to set forth the New Testament method of training those whom God has called to his work.... All theological institutes and missionary training schools are run too much on the theoretical plan, which is detrimental to spirituality and tends to fill the head and empty the heart. In ninety-nine cases out of a hundred a man goes into a missionary training school or theological institute a thousand times better fitted to win souls than he comes out.... It is the special duty of pastors to encourage, and care for, and instruct young workers. Good workers are the natural fruit of an able pastor and a spiritual church.[12]

Those who have had no formal ministerial education are understandably reluctant to place a value on such training. Callen says that almost no pastors had a college degree in 1917 when Anderson Bible Training School was launched.[13] A General Ministerial Assembly resolution passed in 1918 argued that a school education should not be required for ordination: "We believe that no effort should be taken to create a sentiment to the effect that young ministers must attend this school in order to secure recognition."[14] Such sentiments continue today. This might lead some of us to conclude that the Church of God rejects formal education for ministry.

Yet there have always been those in the Church of God who, seeing the value of formal education for Christian ministry, worked to

---

11. Warner and Riggle, *Cleansing the Sanctuary*, 380.

12. D. Otis Teasley, *Gospel Trumpet*, April 6, 1905, 1, cited by Callen, *Preparing for Service*, 16.

13. Callen, *Preparing for Service*, 27.

14. Ibid., 28.

establish institutions of higher education. D. S. Warner himself participated in the founding of a Christian college as early as 1876.[15] This happened before the birth of the Church of God reformation movement
in 1881. The vision of a Church of God ministerial training school
developed at Grand Junction, Michigan, in the 1890s. The death of D.
S. Warner interrupted the implementation of this vision.[16]

One of the earliest ministers to take a strong position in support
of formal education was H. A. Brooks. In 1912, Brooks wrote in the
Gospel Trumpet,

> To the ignorant and unlearned, the advantages of education
> are unknown. There is a sentiment in the minds of many re-
> ligious people against education. We need not hesitate to say
> that such a sentiment can come from only one source, and
> that is the opposite of education—ignorance and illiteracy.
>
> Surely there is no evil in knowing how to do and say things
> well. Yet the unlearned maintain that it tends to pride and
> worldliness. This is not so; and indeed it is true that there
> are many more self-conceited people among the uneducated
> than there are among the learned.[17]

The earliest efforts at operating schools for ministerial preparation could be found in our missionary homes. In the early decades of
the Church of God, these missionary homes were established in cities
across the United States as focal points for evangelism and a place for
itinerant preachers to find lodging. Young persons would migrate to
these urban homes to join the workforce of the Kingdom. Training became increasingly regulated, until schools were formed, some of which
developed into colleges. The first such effort was in Chicago in 1895.
A school was operating in the New York missionary home as early as

---

15. Ibid., 12.

16. Ibid., 14.

17. Brooks, "Advantages and Value of Education," 4–5.

1909. A. F. Gray helped launch the Spokane missionary home in 1904, out of which later came the school that was the predecessor of Warner Pacific College.[18] The short-lived Kansas City Bible Training School was founded in 1919 out of that city's missionary home. However, the missionary homes began to decline by 1910.[19] Callen notes a correlation between the rise of colleges and the shift from "flying messengers" to local pastors.[20] With the decrease of itinerant preachers, the missionary homes became obsolete, and colleges arose as the primary medium of higher education in the Church of God.

Nearly a dozen colleges and universities have been established in North America to prepare ministerial leadership for the Church of God. Anderson University began in 1917 as a Bible training school for *Gospel Trumpet* workers in Anderson, Indiana. J. T. Wilson was the founding principal of this school and later launched a short-lived school in Texas called Warner Memorial University. WMU was started in 1929 and failed in the midst of the Great Depression. H. C. Gardner left Anderson Bible Training School in 1924 to establish Alberta Bible Training Institute in 1933. This school is now known as Gardner College in Camrose, Alberta. After a previous effort failed, Pacific Bible College was established in Spokane, Washington, in 1937. This college continues in Portland, Oregon, as Warner Pacific College.

A School of Theology was launched alongside Anderson College in 1950 and continues as a part of the university. Also launched in 1950 was West Indies Theological College. Nellie Olson went from Anderson to launch Jamaica School of Theology. Gulf-Coast Bible College was established in Houston, Texas, in 1953 and continues as Mid-American Christian University in Oklahoma City. Arlington College was established in Long Beach, California, in 1954 and later merged with several other colleges to form Azusa Pacific College. A school established for the training of Southern black pastors in Mississippi

---

18. Callen, *Preparing for Service*, 18–19.
19. Ibid.
20. Ibid., 19–20.

in 1961 later moved to Kendleton, Texas, and became known as Bay Ridge Christian College. Warner Southern College was established in Lake Wales, Florida, in 1968 to prepare ministers for the southeastern United States.[21]

Because of the visionary thinking of Church of God leaders, colleges are serving across the United States and beyond. These colleges have developed not only to prepare persons for ministry, but also for education, business, and a variety of other vocations. Not only can a person pursue a baccalaureate degree, but two colleges offer master's degrees and the seminary offers a doctorate. Individuals sensing a call to ministry have the option of studying Bible, theology, and ministry without having to enroll in a college which teaches beliefs foreign to the Church of God.

As noted earlier, the Church of God has developed a *Credentials Manual* to encourage the establishment of consistent policies throughout the United States. Since the authority to grant ordination usually lies with regional assemblies, some differences still remain between the ordination standards of various regions. The *Credentials Manual* states:

> If ordination is to be honored by God and respected by the church and the world, it must not serve as the primary basis for the minister's recognition, but rather as acknowledgement of what God obviously has done and intends through the life of a called, committed, and gifted ministerial servant.[22]

Ordination is not the basis of ministry, but rather provides the church's recognition of the calling of God.

The *Credentials Manual* proposes three educational tracks for persons preparing for ministry in the Church of God. The preferred track includes not only a baccalaureate degree, but also a master of divinity seminary degree. Two alternative tracks can also lead to ordination for

---

21. Ibid., 23, 30, 77.

22. Flynn et al, *Credentials Manual,* sec. 2.24

persons who are unable to complete such rigorous academic training. (This provision is surely also a concession to those who resist higher requirements.)

ORDINATION IS FOR THOSE WHO ARE COMMIT-TED TO ADEQUATE EDUCATION FOR THE MINIS-TERIAL PROFESSION.

Early in its history the Church of God recognized the need for ministerial preparation. Both history and experience re-inforce the need for a prepared ministry in order to function effectively in today's complex world. That preparation not only focuses on the beginning period of entering ministry, but also extends throughout one's ministry—regardless of degrees carried. While affirming that God provides divine gifts to called servants for ministry, it is likewise affirmed that refinement is always needed and that other abilities and skills must be developed.

Therefore, there should be a formal structure of ministerial preparation to enable the fuller presence of what the New Testament requires (I Timothy 3 and Titus 1). This biblical requirement includes a divine call, a divine empowerment to help enable the call, emotional and spiritual maturity, and a program of comprehensive studies to better inform God's call to ministry.

It is strongly recommended that all Church of God minis-try attain a seminary education or its equivalent. However, the diversity of circumstances out of which Church of God ministers respond to God's call necessitates that considerable flexibility be allowed in ministerial preparation. Because cir-cumstances such as those of the bivocational minister or the minister called in later life may affect how one pursues education, several options are offered.[23]

Students who pursue a seminary degree are invited to begin the credentialing process while in school. Students who have completed a baccalaureate degree but have not enrolled in seminary are offered a second track. (This track is especially suited for those whose baccalaureate degree included a ministerial major, as at a Bible college.) A third track is offered for persons with little or no college education.[24]

During the credentialing process, a candidate's ministerial work should be supervised by an experienced minister who mentors the candidate.

Neither supervision nor the supervisor should be seen as threats by the supervised minister. Both are intended as a means of support whereby a minister may be assisted in the pursuit of maximum effectiveness in ministry. Both are intended to provide, in part, for the security of a minister during the transitional time of necessary equipping for ministry. Both are intended to provide for the security of ministerial integrity and congregational prosperity by requiring credible spiritual, emotional, moral, and technical preparation for professional ministry.[25]

A formal regimen of ministerial education can develop several skills useful to a pastor. These include critical thinking, communication skills, biblical scholarship, theological development, and ministry methodology.

The effective minister must have well developed skills in *critical thinking*. Fads and opinions abound in the areas of biblical studies, theology, and ministry practices. The minister must sift through these opinions to

---

23. Ibid., sec. 2.15
24. Ibid.
25. Ibid., sec. 3.21

astutely determine the best choices for the local church. A formal education enables the minister to see through faulty arguments that might otherwise be convincing. Some ministers who prize their lack of education are unaware of the way they have been influenced by sermons they have heard and articles they have read. Effective ministry requires the ability to analyze arguments well and separate the wheat from the chaff to determine which statements are valid.

The effective minister must master the art of *communication*. Writing skills are best honed in a formal educational setting. Rhetoric and oratory have always been central components of a liberal arts education. Proclaiming the gospel requires the very best in written and verbal communication skills. This is especially true in an age when education is available to so many. The minister who is unable to communicate effectively will be a stumbling block to those who might otherwise respond favorably to the gospel. Some people seem to have the gift of gab, but all ministers can benefit from a process of observation and experimentation under supervision as they develop the art of public speaking. Even those who otherwise cannot pursue academic studies should sit under a master in homiletics to improve their skill in preaching.

Biblical *scholarship* is vital to pastoral ministry. Some seem to think that understanding the Bible is as simple as reading what it says and making application to current issues. But ill-informed persons have often drawn erroneous conclusions because they used words in different ways than intended in the Scripture. Sound biblical interpretation is a skill that must be learned. A reader can better interpret the Bible by studying the historical contexts in which the Bible was written. Interpretation is further enhanced when the reader understands the various types of literature found in the Bible and the differences between its literary genres. Before we can rightly discern the meaning of a biblical passage for us, we must discern the original intent of the author. This is the work of *exegesis*. Having determined (as best as possible) the original intent of a biblical text, we must cross the millennia to determine how the text speaks to us today. This is the task of *hermeneutics*. The trained biblical interpreter is familiar with a variety of approaches to hermeneutics and the strengths and weaknesses of each. At all times, hermeneutics must be restrained by sound exegesis. In other words, a limited number of valid options are available for a preacher's interpretation of a given text.[26]

The minister must be well trained in *theological thinking*. Education seeks to go beyond mere rote recitation of "the right answers" to a complex exploration of theological issues. Study of church history provides a framework for interacting with theological ideas that continually arise. How much better it would be if all of our ministers understood the historical precedents for divisive theological controversies such as those we are experiencing over tongues and end times. Rather than being blown by every wind of doctrine, ministers must be well-grounded in classic Christian thinking.

The effective minister knows a variety of *ministry methods* and has developed a philosophy of ministry in a coherent manner. Without proper education, a minister might be able to emulate the methods of a mentor, but these methods may not work in another time or place. Success in ministry requires a variety of skills in preaching, Christian education, evangelism, discipleship, administration, and pastoral care. Few mentoring pastors are gifted so broadly that they can equip a young minister in all the areas required. Ministry methodology changes continually, making it even harder for the pastor working in the field to keep up. A well-designed process of formal education can equip a minister for a lifetime of service far better than a string of conferences about the latest and greatest ministry ideas.

There are still some who advocate that persons can best do ministry without the structured training provided by theological schools. It cannot be denied that some persons have given exceptional service in ministry without conventional preparation. But these anecdotes do not prove that this should be the norm. There is great value in learning ministry as an apprentice. But even a pastoral mentor has a significant handicap: No working pastor can stay current on all the areas required

---

26. For an introductory discussion of these issues, read Fee and Stuart, *How to Read the Bible*, 13–44.

for ministerial preparation while also leading a church. On the other hand, a professor can concentrate attention on a limited field, whether Bible, church history, theology, ethics, religion, social sciences, preaching, administration, evangelism, Christian education, or other ministry trends. Certainly, there is a danger that a faculty member may become isolated in the ivory tower of academia. The best solution is a partnership between school and church. At Warner Pacific College, ministry students are required to engage in ministry under the supervision of qualified ministers while pursuing a rigorous program of academic study. This enables students to prepare for ministry with a comprehensive program of study and a mentored process of practical experience. Even D. Otis Teasley acknowledged the value of this: "There are two great methods of training; either of which, taken alone, is not God's plan. These are the theoretical and experiential methods."[27] Another approach is for clusters of ministers to work together as they prepare for service in an academic setting.[28]

We need to make the most of our colleges and credentialing authorities. Every congregation should include at least one of the church colleges in its mission budget. Church of God families should consider our own colleges when planning the educational path for their children.[29] Persons serving in ministry should take advantage of continuing-education resources available to them. Churches seeking a pastor should consult with their area credential committees to screen candidates, making sure that they talk with people who are well-prepared for the work of ministry.

The lack of ministerial training is not just an evangelical problem; it is a Church of God problem. We must outgrow our headstrong spirit

---

27. D. O. Teasley, *Gospel Trumpet*, April 6, 1905, 1. Callen deleted this line when he quoted from this article (*Preparing for Service*, 16).

28. One such design is described in McNeal, *Revolution in Leadership*.

29. Research indicates that when Christian students enroll in a state university, over half lose their faith by the time of graduation, and students who enroll in a church-based college from another church tradition tend to follow that college's tradition after graduation. If we want our children to remain in the Church of God, we must support our own colleges.

of independence and join together in the task of training people for ministry, so that we can "become mature, attaining to the whole measure of the fullness of Christ" (Eph 4:13).

FOR FURTHER STUDY

Flynn, Jeannette, et al. Credentials Manual of the Church of God. Revised Ed. Anderson, IN: Church of God Ministries, 2004.

Callen, Barry L. *Preparing for Service: A History of Higher Education in the Church of God.* Anderson, IN: Warner Press, 1988.

Oden, Thomas C. *Pastoral Theology: Essentials of Ministry.* San Francisco: HarperSanFranscisco, 1983. See chap. 1, "Becoming a Minister."

McNeal, Reggie. *Revolution in Leadership: Training Apostles for Tomorrow's Church.* Nashville: Abingdon, 1998.

QUESTIONS FOR DISCUSSION

1. What stories do you know of people studying at Church of God colleges? (Stories may include people outside the group.)

2. Brainstorm a policy for ministerial preparation and ordination, including academic preparation, spiritual preparation, mentoring, and credentialing. If you were making the rules for persons preparing to enter pastoral ministry in the Church of God, what would you require?

6.

What's the Difference between Christian Faith and American Religion?

THE CIRCUS tent was packed with over a thousand voters enjoying barbeque. Red, white, and blue bunting surrounded the platform. A southern gospel quartet had regaled the gathering with patriotic songs for a half hour before the speeches began. A uniformed honor guard of soldiers from the army, air force, navy, marines, and coast guard had led a salute to the local residents who were serving in Iraq and Afghanistan. Voter guidelines had been distributed and careful instruction given on which candidates held views that made them the right choice. Now a local pastor was whipping the crowd to a frenzy: "With your help, we're gonna win this election for JEEEZUS!"

In the past quarter century, the Christian Right has developed a political machine that has effectively mobilized Christians to vote for candidates who are pledged to support conservative social values. Abortion is often a leading issue for this movement. Less visible is a pro-business agenda and limited interest in civil rights. Foreign policy is expected to maintain global hegemony for the United States with a hawkish posture toward anyone who threatens American interests. Loyalty to country and faithfulness to God are portrayed as interchangeable values. With rare exceptions, one political party is seen as harmonious with Christian values while the other represents immorality and iniquity.

A group is rising in strength among the Christian Right that has very different beliefs and expectations than traditional evangelicalism.[1] This group is known as Christian Reconstructionism. The classic evangelical

---

1. I am using *evangelical* in a restricted sense, as explained in the Introduction and Appendix B.

worldview tends to be pessimistic about the world around us, expecting continued decline until Jesus returns, but Christian Reconstruction expects to reform society within history through social and political action. While most modern evangelicals tend to be premillennial in their eschatology, Christian Reconstructionists adopt a more postmillennial view.[2] They hope to alter American law so that it will conform to the Ten Commandments. This movement arose out of the Reformed tradition in the 1970s. Some Reconstructionists promote home schooling and Christian private schooling in order to prepare children for a radical transformation of American government. Even Ralph Reed of the Christian Coalition describes Christian Reconstructionism as "an authoritarian ideology that threatens the most basic civil liberties of a free and democratic society." Gary DeMar and Gary North are two of the better-known writers from this group. Leading evangelicals Pat Robertson, Donald Wildmon, D. James Kennedy, Tim LeHaye, and Robert Dugan have been connected with Reconstructionist views.[3]

Christian Reconstructionists dispute the values of other conservative Christians at several points. Where Christians in the Anabaptist[4] tradition oppose capital punishment, Reconstructionists hope to apply the death penalty to quell a variety of social problems (prostitution, adultery, homosexuality, witchcraft, and heresy), as prescribed in the Law of Moses. They would restrict the role of women in society, in a reversion to patriarchal gender roles.[5] Such extremism runs contrary to the centrist social policies that have been traditionally advocated by the Church of God.

Even evangelical Christians who are not Reconstructionists may be unable to distinguish the difference between biblical Christianity and

---

2. Chapter three is devoted to a discussion on millennial views.

3. "Theonomy and Christian Reconstructionism," http://www.geocities.com/Athens/Academy/2850/Theonomy.html. (accessed November 9, 2005).

4. I will be discussing the Anabaptist tradition and its relationship with the Church of God.

5. B.A. Robinson, "Dominionism (A.K.A. Christian Reconstructionism, Dominion Theology, and Theonomy)," Ontario Consultants on Religious Tolerance, http://www.religioustolerance.org/reconstr.htm. (accessed November 9, 2005).

American civil religion. American civil religion is a set of social and political beliefs which have long been a part of the culture of the United States but are not rooted in the Bible. For example, some people have the erroneous belief that the principle of self-sufficiency, God helps those that help themselves, comes from the Bible.[6] Where the core principle of Christianity is the atonement, American civil religion is rooted in capitalism. American civil religion stresses self-sufficiency, the idea that all persons can pick themselves up by their own bootstraps. From this perspective, social welfare is wrong because it amounts to taking money from wage earners and giving it to lazy people. American civil religion tends to be nationalistic, seeing the United States as the greatest nation on earth. It seeks to use foreign aid as a tool to further American interests throughout the world. From this perspective, America is the nation blessed by God because of its unique virtue. While many evangelicals are comfortable with American civil religion, this set of beliefs runs contrary to the Church of God heritage.

This movement is rooted in a tradition with values that diverge from the political agenda of American civil religion. Church of God tradition flows from the Radical Reformation (also known as the Anabaptist movement) of the sixteenth century. The term *Anabaptist* should not be confused with familiar denominational names such as Southern Baptists or Freewill Baptists. The name Anabaptist alludes to the practice of baptizing only adult believers instead of practicing infant baptism. Another significant element of this tradition is its commitment to peacemaking or pacifism. But perhaps the greatest influence of the Anabaptist tradition on American culture is its doctrine of separation of church and state. More than any other denomination, the Mennonites represent the Anabaptist tradition today. This "third wing"[7] of the Protestant Reformation shaped the earliest days of the Church of God as people from Brethren churches "came out" of these Anabaptist churches to identify with the Reformation Movement.

---

6. The source is actually *Poor Richard's Almanac* by Benjamin Franklin.

7. After the Lutheran and Reformed wings of the Protestant Reformation.

This lineage has shaped the Church of God in significant ways. Church of God leader and peace activist John Albright identifies the Church of God as a "peace church."

> D. S. Warner and E. E. Byrum, the first two editors of *The Gospel Trumpet*, our official publication for over 80 years, were committed pacifists. They strongly denounced all violence and war.
>
> This is our heritage. Historically, the Church of God has been known as a Peace Church. In interdenominational directories, along with Quakers, Mennonites, Brethren, and others, we were listed as a Peace Church.
>
> Today, the Church of God supports conscientious objectors as well as men and women in the military. We have chaplains serving in the armed forces. It's viewed as a personal conscience matter. But we should remember our heritage. And more importantly, we owe it to the Prince of Peace to seek peace first, and always be searching for alternatives to war.[8]

Church of God historian Merle Strege discusses this same background and concludes that the Church of God is not a peace church in the same mold at the Mennonites, because the Church of God has always included a diversity of views on war and peace.[9] But the heritage of the Church of God has included Anabaptist themes that set us apart from other churches in the Holiness Movement. What is the implication of our Anabaptist legacy for the Church of God?

In a discussion on capital punishment, the nineteenth-century evangelist W. G. Schell provides an example of the Anabaptist spirit that informed early Church of God thinking:

---

8. Albright, "Adam Was a Pacifist."

9. Strege, *I Saw the Church*, 117–21, 130, 306–7.

I am constrained to reverence the political powers and to uphold them because they are instituted by God, but I cannot be induced to believe that all their laws are by inspiration and therefore must believe that even the political powers may, sometimes be mistaken. Their laws are made by fallible men, and we should not feel ourselves under obligation to uphold a law that we cannot conscientiously believe to be correct. We should be subject to the laws although they be erroneous and unjust, when they do not interfere with our duty to God; but there is no just reason why we should not feel ourselves at liberty to cry out boldly against a law enacted by men that is contrary to the sentiments of that perfect law revealed unto us by our Savior. [10]

This paragraph was reprinted in a 1917 statement by the Executive Committee of the Missionary Board of the Church of God, and was published by the Church of God Peace Fellowship in their Spring 2005 newsletter. It represents early Church of God teaching on the relationship of the church and government.[11]

Some of the earliest expressions from Church of God writers about war came in the context of the Spanish-American War. In 1898, articles in the *Gospel Trumpet* raised questions about whether war was a proper action and whether a Christian in the army should desert. The paper's answer to the question, "Would it be right for a holy man of God to go as a soldier?" was, "Emphatically no."[12]

Strege notes that anti-war statements of the *Gospel Trumpet* which began during the Spanish-American War continued into World War I.[13] A 1907 letter to the editor about participation in war was answered with a quote of Romans 13:10 and the question, "What would Jesus

---

10. Schell, *Better Testament,* 341–42.

11. Smith, Byrum, and Phelps, "Teaching of the Church of God."

12. "Deserting the Army," *Gospel Trumpet,* February 10, 1898, 4.; also E. E. Byrum, "Should We Go to War?"

13. Strege, *I Saw the Church,* 117–19.

do?"[14] A similar letter to the editor in 1909 produced the answer, "I should refuse to go to war or to obey an officer's command to shoot anyone. We are followers of the 'Prince of peace' and 'the weapon of our warfare are not carnal.'"[15] The second *Gospel Trumpet* editor, E. E. Byrum, supported Christians serving in the armed forces as noncombatants. In one of the last editions printed while Byrum was editor, an article opened by saying that a Christian could rightly serve in the military but must not participate in the shedding of blood:

> War is cruel, and devastation, with foul murder, disease, destruction of property, breaking up of homes, follows in its track, leaving the land strewn with the dead bodies of the best talent the country can afford; and starving widows and fatherless children continue to partake of the miseries that follow in the wake of war. There are no humane bullets.
>
> Jesus Christ said, 'Love your enemies.' He did not say shoot them.[16]

While Byrum advised that Christians should not participate in battle, he left open the possibility that some Christians might do so in obedience to their country's call.

As public opinion in the United States turned toward participation in World War I, the *Gospel Trumpet* ran an article opposing the trend to incorporate military training into educational programs and gearing up for arms production.[17] A 1917 article in the *Gospel Trumpet* spoke against the taking of human lives in war and asked that readers stop mailing in questions about how to respond to a draft.[18] The *Gospel*

---

14. "Questions Answered," *Gospel Trumpet,* May 30, 1907, 9.
15. "Questions Answered," *Gospel Trumpet,* Apr. 1, 1909, 9.
16. "Is It Wrong to Be a Soldier?" *Gospel Trumpet,* April 27, 1916, 3.
17. "Reaction Against Preparedness," *Gospel Trumpet*, May 11, 1916, 16.
18. "Our Attitude toward War," *Gospel Trumpet*, April 26, 1917, 12.

Trumpet recognized a growing sentiment of patriotism in the United States, yet opposed war and killing.[19]

In 1917, the Executive Committee of the Missionary Board of the Church of God published the following statement of pacifism:

> As a minister of the church of God. I, in agreement with my fellow ministers, hereby declare:
>
> That I believe in being a loyal citizen and servant of the Government under which I live in so far as its requirements do not conflict with my duty to God as enforced by the law of my conscience.
>
> That...it is contrary to my religious convictions as a follower of Christ for me to take human life. My religion and my conscience forbid my taking up arms for the slaughter of my fellowmen.[20]

While the passion for pacifism faded after the editorships of E. E. Byrum and F. G. Smith, there have been ongoing Church of God expressions of the Anabaptist distaste for war. Four times the General Assembly has passed resolutions objecting to military conscription (1928, 1932, 1947, and 1966).[21] As the fourth editor of *Gospel Trumpet*, C.E. Brown educated the Church of God on its own Anabaptist heritage.[22]

Strege argues that pacifism has been a minority position among the Church of God. While occasional statements of advocacy have been made, the *Gospel Trumpet* usually has held an ambivalent position on pacifism.[23] Strege says Church of God people generally participated in World War II at the same rate as others and that there were very few conscientious objectors. He further says that conscientious objectors

19. "Patriotism and Conscience," *Gospel Trumpet*, May 17, 1917, 16.
20. Smith, Byrum, and Phelps, "Teaching of the Church of God."
21. Callen, *Following the Light*, 233–34, 241–42.
22. Strege, *I Saw the Church*, 210–222.
23. Ibid., 121.

faced disapproval from the Church of God community in at least a few instances.[24] Strege argues that expressions of anti-war protest among the Church of God during the Vietnam War were influenced more by the contemporary culture than the Anabaptist heritage of the Church of God.[25] In the late 1970s and 1980s, an alternative Church of God journal arose titled *Colloquium*. This journal spoke as "an antidote to middle America's blend of patriotism and religion."[26] The conflict over pacifism is illustrated by the fact that Dean Russell Olt of Anderson College was a leading pacifist while Charles Wilson would go from Anderson to be Secretary of Defense for the Eisenhower administration.[27] Strege comments on this irony, noting that the campus of Anderson University has buildings named for both of these men within a hundred yards of each other.[28]

As pacifism faded from the power center of the editorship of *Gospel Trumpet*, a group of ministers organized as the Church of God Peace Fellowship. The first efforts of this group were led by Russell Olt, Adam W. Miller, Carl Kardatzke, and others in the 1930s. The group was inactive for years before reasserting itself in 1966 under the leadership of Robert J. Hazen, H.L. Nelson, Val Clear, Mack Caldwell, Hollis Pistole, and others..

In 1960, Robert Hazen wrote a letter to the editor of the *Gospel Trumpet,* objecting to a photo of soldiers with an article, "Serving God in the Military Service," published earlier that year. Hazen acknowledged that pacifists were a distinct minority (a "very, very small minority") in the Church of God.[29] The article which provoked Hazen's response made no reference to the possibility of a soldier killing another.

---

24. Strege, *I Saw the Church*, 133n57; see also John W. V. Smith, *Quest for Holiness and Unity*, 308.

25. Strege, *I Saw the Church*, 307.

26. "Forum," *Colloquium,* November–December 1979, 8; cited in Strege, *I Saw the Church*, 331–32.

27. Callen, *Preparing for Service*, 37.

28. Strege, "Demise of a Peace Church."

29. *Gospel Trumpet*, March 20, 1960, 16.

It simply warned of the temptations of alcohol and sexuality in the military lifestyle. The article argued that a soldier could live the Christian lifestyle and provide ministry while in the military.[30] Editor Harold L. Philips responded with an editorial holding a moderate stance and suggesting that those who pay taxes to fund a war are no less culpable than those who wear the uniform.[31]

Robert Hazen has been a vocal advocate for pacifism among Church of God leaders serving in Michigan and Canada. Hazen observes American Christians' confusion over the connection between patriotism and Christian faith.

> The U.S. often links together patriotism, war, and Christian faith. Not so in Canada, where I live. Here it is not unpatriotic to speak against the government's military action or non-action. The U.S. ties patriotism to supporting war.

> Canadian youth visiting U.S. churches wonder about the U.S. and Christian flags displayed in some sanctuaries. Does that mean keep the church and state separate, except at the point of patriotism?[32]

Humorist Sam Collins recently provided a reminder of our Anabaptist heritage in calling us to eschew entanglement of the church with political parties.

> Traditionally, the Church of God has said that fidelity to God lies in the condition of the human heart, not in denominational or political affiliations. I am convinced that we have a role to play in fostering reconciliation and helping heal the land. But it is a role we will be ill-equipped to play if we succumb to the temptation to adopt the manner and methods of polarizing political action groups.

---

30. Johnson, "Serving God in the Military Service."

31. *Gospel Trumpet*, March 20, 1960, 3.

32. Hazen, "My Dual Citizenship."

Our role is to be leaven in society rather than to embrace any particular political agenda within society. What our nation requires are calming voices that speak from a place of spiritual centeredness—peacemakers and reconcilers rather than partisans and dogmatic Dobermans who growl warnings and bare their fangs. What we need are fewer withering blowtorches of self-righteousness and more illuminating candles softly sharing Christ's warmth and light in the cold, dark corners of our estrangement.[33]

Despite these examples of Anabaptist spirit, the Church of God has never been a peace church like the Mennonites or Quakers. As Strege concludes, the Church of God "was a church that had the head for pacifism but not the character, or heart."[34] Still, the Church of God has carried a spirit very different than that of evangelicals who tend to be patriotic, pro-war, and staunchly Republican.

A leading voice among contemporary Anabaptists beyond the Church of God is Jim Wallis. In the introduction to his recent book *God's Politics*, Wallis declares:

God is not partisan. God is not a Republican or a Democrat. When either party tries to politicize God or co-opt religious communities to further political agendas, it makes a terrible mistake. The best contribution of religion is precisely not to be ideologically predictable nor loyally partisan. Both parties, and the nation, must let the prophetic voice of religion be heard. Faith must be free to challenge both the Right and the Left from a consistent moral ground.[35]

Whose side is God on? When preparing for the great battle of Jericho to begin the conquest of the Promised Land, Joshua encountered an angel. Joshua asked the angel whether he was with Israel or the

---

33. Collins, Sam. "Candles or Blowtorches?"
34. Strege, "Demise of a Peace Church," 140.
35. Wallis, *God's Politics*, xiv.

enemy. The angel's response was, "Neither." Instead he identified himself as "commander of the army of the LORD" (Josh 5:13–14). Joshua responded appropriately in worship. Too often we try to position God as being on our side. If we are wise, we will ask whether we are on God's side.

The Gospels show no propensity for Jesus to get involved in political affairs, even though the Romans oppressed the people of Israel. The Zealot party sought to engage in political upheaval as a service to God. Though Jesus called a Zealot to be one of the Twelve, he never voiced support of their agenda. When the Pharisees and the Herodians confronted him with a political dilemma, Jesus deftly deflected their question with an answer that refused to take sides (Matt 22:15–21).

Many have difficulty reconciling the message of peace embodied in Jesus with the fervor to make war displayed by some Americans. Jesus says, "Love your enemies and pray for those who persecute you" (Matt 5:44). To a world that only understands self-protection, Jesus says, "Do not resist an evil person. If someone strikes you on the right cheek, turn to him the other also" (Matt 5:39). After Peter displayed a violent response to aggression, Jesus commanded, "Put your sword back in its place...for all who draw the sword will die by the sword" (Matt 26:52).

For instance, the war in Iraq presents a challenge for Christians. For some, anything other than fervent support for the war is a denial of patriotism and a demonstration of lack of Christian commitment. Others are troubled by intervention in another country's political system, the failure to find weapons of mass destruction (WMD), the loss of life (both American and Iraqi), and incidences like the torture at Abu Graib prison. The Church of God must avoid becoming a political hack for either the Right or the Left. We are called to stand for righteousness and to speak prophetically without becoming entangled with political organizations and agendas.

The role of the church is to stand apart from the political structure as a prophetic voice, not to be co-opted by a political party seeking power. Even in the Old Testament, at a time when the political leader was rightly believed to be God's anointed king, prophets arose to speak the Word of God to the king. At times, we may be required to practice civil disobedience to resist the government when it acts in defiance to God's will and justice. By identifying with one political party because we favor its stance on certain social issues, the church may ignore other issues where that same party is out of step with biblical values. The church is not the handmaiden of any political party. Rather, the church must hold all political parties accountable for their promises and their actions.

Some would suggest that an American flag should not be displayed in church sanctuaries during worship services. This is an area over which Christians will disagree strongly. An Anabaptist view might be expressed in this way: Our gatherings for worship are dedicated to the King of Kings, and his symbol is the cross. Displays of flags on the platform and singing patriotic songs during worship distract from the rightful object of our worship. Patriotism has its place, but not in God's sanctuary during times of holy worship. Hazen's comments suggest that such a mixing of patriotism and faith is unique to the culture of the United States. Some Church of God congregations, sensitive to the issue of nationalism, only display the American flag on occasions when a missions emphasis calls for displaying an array of national flags. Others in the Church of God would reject this viewpoint, seeing no conflict between patriotism and Christian worship.

Perhaps modern evangelicals have sold their soul for a mess of pottage. Holiness requires us to come out from all unrighteousness. Where our government rules in righteousness, we do well to commend its policies. Where our government or a political party is in conflict with God's will, we are constrained to obey the King. While Christians hold divergent opinions on peace and war, we must not blindly follow our government without asking questions about the justice of its military and political actions. While we are loyal citizens of our country, our first obligation is to God.

Church of God Peace Fellowship Web site. www.peacecog.com.

Strege, Merle. *I Saw the Church*. Anderson, IN: Warner Press, 2002. See pp. 117–21, 130, 306-7.

Strege, Merle. "The Demise (?) of a Peace Church: The Church of God (Anderson), Pacifism, and Civil Religion." *Mennonite Quarterly Report*, 65, no. 2 (April 1991): 128–40.

Strege, Merle. "An Uncertain Voice for Peace." In *Proclaim Peace*, edited by Theron F. Schlabach and Richard T. Hughes, 115–127. Urbana, IL: University of Chicago Press, 1997.

Wallis, Jim. *God's Politics: Why the Right Gets It Wrong, and the Left Doesn't Get It*. San Francisco: HarperSanFrancisco, 2005.

QUESTIONS FOR DISCUSSION

1. What leads some Christians to be pacifists while others are committed to a "just war"?

2. Is serving in the military morally equivalent to being a taxpaying and voting citizen in a country that engages in war?

3. Should Christians be involved in the political process? Why or why not?

4. How can a church speak to moral issues without been compromised by political agendas?

5. Some seek to conform American law to the Ten Commandments. Is this a good idea? Why or why not?

6. Does Christian conviction inform the doctrine of the separation of church and state? Why or why not?

7. Do you believe it is appropriate to display the American flag in a church sanctuary? Why or why not?

8. Can a Christian be a patriotic citizen? If not, why not? If so, how does one balance loyalties to God and country?

9. Hickson contrasts biblical Christianity with American civil religion. Do you see a difference? If so, where are the points of contrast?

7.

Has Right to Life Gone Overboard?

TERRI SCHIAVO became a cause celebre in the first decade of the twenty-first century. Her life illustrated the dilemma which advances in medical technology can pose to simplistic moral thinking. Terri had spent fifteen years caught in limbo between life and death. For seven years, a legal battle had ensued between her husband Michael, who wanted to discontinue her artificial life support, and her parents, who insisted she was not beyond hope. This battle was joined by the press and by elected officials in Tallahassee, Florida, and Washington, DC.

Terri had collapsed on February 25, 1990, when the flow of oxygen to her brain had been interrupted, causing brain damage. Some alleged that Terri had succumbed to an eating disorder; others alleged her husband Michael had abused her. A medical malpractice award of $1 million was largely consumed by legal and medical expenses. The remaining $300,000 may have been the root of her husband's conflict with her parents, Mary and Robert Schindler. Terri died on March 31, 2005, in Pinellas Park, Florida, after her feeding tube was removed on March 18. An autopsy documented irreversible brain damage, showing that she was blind and had lost half of her brain mass.[1]

Terri Schiavo's struggle dominated television, newspaper, and magazine coverage for months. It became the focus of heated debates on the Internet. Roles seemed to be reversed as political conservatives called for increased government intrusion while liberals argued for personal privacy rights. Both sides were clearly trying to protect their own hidden agendas, such as the right to abortion and the right to life. It was

---

1. Campo-Flores, "Legacy of Terri Schiavo."

hard to find information that was not laden with emotional hype. The language of demagoguery called Michael a "murderer." Some accused him of being motivated by the desire for money, yet he declined at least one offer of one million dollars to surrender his wife's guardianship.

Perhaps we should back up a bit and consider the implications of this case for Christian morality.

I speak as a Christian who holds pro-life values. While pastor of a church in northern California, I served on the board of directors of a crisis pregnancy center and a maternity home. During my last two years, I was the chairman of the board of the CPC. We provided free pregnancy tests and educational services for women who might go elsewhere to get an abortion. The maternity home provided shelter for women who needed a place to go during their pregnancy, as well as job training and assistance in preparing for motherhood or adoption.

I am disturbed by the way abortion has become simply another method of birth control for those who have been irresponsible with their sexuality. I am also concerned about the way that the Supreme Court's *Roe v. Wade* decision opened other doors to a low regard for human life. Some babies are aborted because tests reveal that they have a genetic disorder. Having parented one of these children, I take the matter rather personally. No child lacks value, regardless of whether the pregnancy was planned or involves a disability. Other babies are aborted because they are not the gender that the parents desire. (I find it ironic that some promote abortion as a matter of women's rights when female babies are far more likely to be aborted than boys, especially in China and India.) The zeal for abortion as a personal right causes some to allow even third-trimester abortions (so-called partial birth abortions). A society so callous to the unborn need only take a short step to practice infanticide, allowing small children to be killed or starved to death because they are not desired. The same low regard for human life has already reared its head in Oregon, which has passed a law permitting physician-assisted suicide. Other states are likely to follow. These developments echo the philosophy of Margaret Sanger, which came to fruition in the Nazi concentration camps. One can easily imagine a scenario in which older adults feel pressured to terminate their own lives because they present a burden to others.

I also speak as one who had to make the painful decision to terminate life support for my own daughter. Melissa was fourteen at the time and had contracted a post-operative staph infection. Melissa had fought painful medical challenges for her entire life. We loved our child and gave her the best chance at life we could. The infection followed the insertion of a pacemaker, which we hoped would help Melissa overcome chronic cardiac arrest. After a successful surgery and recovery, the staph bacteria entered a chest suture and followed the pacemaker wire to become a major infection in her heart. This infection threatened to break loose and block an artery. Melissa spent a month in intensive care as we pursued intravenous antibiotic therapy. She was in a coma most of that time. While the therapy was able to kill the staph infection, most of her organs failed in the process. We chose to terminate Melissa's life support only after pursuing every treatment available and reaching the conclusion that death was inevitable.

One question we asked in making the decision was, How long might Melissa live without life support? We were reminded of the famous case of Karen Ann Quinlan.[2] Our doctor's opinion was that Melissa's death would be very swift without the medications that were being pumped into her veins. We made what we believed was the right decision, and Melissa lived ninety minutes apart from the machinery. That time gave us the opportunity to hold our daughter in the presence of her extended family. While this brought us real anguish, we believed we had accepted the best outcome available. We chose to be with our daughter as she died rather than get a 2:00 AM phone call informing us that Melissa had died alone. It was an awesomely memorable experience. I can only hope that my death will also occur in the company of those I love.

As we confronted the decisions around Melissa's life and death, one thought guided me: just because we have the ability to do something doesn't make it right. Our sophisticated technology has taken us into

---

2. Quinlan was disconnected from a resuscitator in 1976 and died in 1985.

a world of ethical dilemmas. We are being confronted with questions that were not raised a century ago, and are today still unknown in much of the world. We can delay death in many cases for extended periods of time, but delaying death may not be the best choice in every case.

If anyone can face death without fear, it should be the Christian. Do we not believe what we say? Are we not convinced that another existence far better than this awaits us beyond death? I can understand how one who does not know God would fear death. I can understand how physicians take death as a personal affront, as though they have failed. But physical death is a natural part of life. In order to provide as good a life as possible, we should use medical science wherever it can combat illness or injury, but we should also accept the fact that death must come eventually to every person.

Let me state this very precisely: allowing death to occur is not the same as hastening death. The removal of a patient's feeding tube is common when death is imminent. If the rhetoric of murder used in the Terri Schiavo case is valid, then we have thousands of murderers in our churches.

I see no moral option in euthanasia. Administering drugs that cause death is an inappropriate use of medical science. On the other hand, one could argue that allowing death to occur is simply an acceptance of reality.[3] Some believe that we are obligated to supply every medical patient with food and water. Here our technology presents another ethical challenge. Without the feeding tube, persons who cannot feed themselves will die of starvation. With the feeding tube, we are forcing food and water into a body that would otherwise not survive. A feeding tube is often necessary to support a patient through post-surgical recovery. But when a patient is in a long-term coma or permanent vegetative state, the same support may be pointless.

---

3. *Christian History & Biography* magazine presented a balanced discussion on the difference between euthanasia and allowing death with references to several Christian authorities. It should be noted that this periodical comes from leading evangelical publisher *Christianity Today*. See Armstrong, "Not a Mercy but a Sin."

We need to consider carefully the ethics of medical costs. Simplistic thinking merely declares that every life has infinite value. But we live in a world of limited resources, and we must decide how those resources will be used. The decision to allocate resources to prolong the life of one person may result in the deaths of several others. Some cases require millions of dollars of care, straining the budgets of the family, hospitals, and insurance companies. Is it right to devote all these resources to extend the life of one who will die in a short time anyway and may not be conscious through this time? Such an effort is unjust if it denies medical care to others simply because they lack medical insurance or are citizens of a poorer country. These dilemmas are unique to American hospitals; people around the world are sent home to die daily.

Already, the ethical morass presented by technology and end-of-life decisions creates painful inconsistencies. One man asked for a DNR (Do Not Resuscitate) order, only to have his family demand that the resident keep him alive long enough for his daughter to arrive.[4] We are now in the position of playing God, setting schedules for our loved one's death to suit our personal convenience. We are only in this predicament because our affluence has given us the ability to make such choices. But we need to think carefully about our perspective on death itself.

The use of pacemakers or ICDs (Implantable Cardioverter Defibrillators) presents other challenges. For example, suppose a patient with a pacemaker has requested a DNR order. Since this device restarts the heart when if stops, does the pacemaker itself countermand the DNR order? If so, should the pacemaker be deactivated?[5] Would doing so constitute murder? Such ethical dilemmas can only multiply as we continue to develop increasingly sophisticated medical technology.

What does the Church of God have to say about these issues of medical ethics? Since the pro-life controversy arose after the legalization of abortion in 1973, we should not expect to find it discussed by

---

4. Brooke, "Bowing to Family Pressure."
5. Morrison, "Next-of-Kin Responses."

early Church of God writers. While some Church of God people have expressed pro-life views, there are certainly others who differ. In the pages that follow, I will attempt to set forth some principles that are faithful to biblical teaching and consistent with the theological heritage of the Church of God.

From the earliest days, the Church of God has emphasized the power of divine healing.[6] Healing was judged an integral part of the salvation provided through Christ. Rather than rely on doctors and medical technology, Church of God people relied on the power of prayer to overcome all kinds of diseases.[7] At times, this practice went to excess. The Church of God moderated this teaching in recognition that illness and death confront even the saints.[8] Over the years, we have learned that God sometimes works through doctors and medical procedures. Still, the current obsession with medical techniques differs markedly from the simple faith of our heritage. Underneath the contemporary attitude of many Christians lies a materialism that sees nothing beyond this life.

Recognizing that Church of God writers lived before the advent of these specific questions, shall we look to see what early teachings of the movement might inform this discussion?

F. G. Smith argued against materialism, saying that a human being is a duality of body and soul.[9] He said, "At death the soul takes its departure from the body to be in a more sacred nearness with the Lord."[10] While advocating prayers for divine healing, Smith said, "We may be sure that the real 'prayer of faith' for perfect healing and restoration cannot be offered when it is to the glory of God to take the person

---

6. The classic Church of God position on divine healing can be found in F. G. Smith, *What the Bible Teaches*, 141–55 and Russell R. Byrum, *Christian Theology*, 488–504.

7. Strege, *I Saw the Church*, 66–74.

8. Ibid., 232–34. In one case, Church of God people were charged with murder for failing to seek medical care leading to the death of Sarah Johnson (Strege, *I Saw the Church*, 91n30).

9. F. G. Smith, *What the Bible Teaches*, 41–42.

10. Ibid., 46. A. F. Gray takes a similar position in *Christian Theology*, 1:243–44.

home to himself."[11] R. R. Byrum picked up on this, saying, "Evidently some are not healed because it is appointed unto man to die and the time has come when God wills that they depart from this life."[12] While some in the Church of God eschewed all use of medical science in his day, Byrum suggested a more open stance.

> How far one may go consistently with faith in God in assisting nature by regulation of diet, employment of various appliances, and other remedial efforts is not stated in the Scriptures. It is a matter to be determined by the judgment and conscience of the one concerned. The Bible has drawn no fine line as to limitations in such instances, and it is useless for men to attempt drawing such a line.[13]

A. F. Gray made it clear that death is inevitable, saying, "A few men have supposed they could escape death, but only those whom God has translated have been able to escape its clutches."[14] While continuing the Church of God teaching on divine healing, Gray made it clear that God does not always heal.[15] He did not see death as the final enemy.

> Does death end all? If for the human race death is the end of all existence, there is nothing future to which we may look. The few who so believe are prone to adapt the policy, "Let us eat, and be merry, for tomorrow we die." However, there are strong reasons for believing that death does not end all and that beyond this life there is a future.[16]

Church of God heritage songs convey the same hope-filled conviction concerning death:

---

11. Ibid., 151.
12. Russell R. Byrum, *Christian Theology*, 496.
13. Ibid., 502.
14. Gray, *Christian Theology*, 1:246.
15. Ibid., 2:101.
16. Ibid., 2:221.

We'll praise the Lord that death's dark valley
    is no longer drear;
The light of Love dispels the shadows,
    Drives away the fear.[17]

When I face death's chilly river,
When upon its brink I stand,
I shall fearless be if Jesus
Leads me gently by the hand.[18]

Death is not our enemy. We have nothing to fear in death. We can trust God to walk us through that stage of life to the life to come. This attitude toward death should inform every Christian's thinking about the use of medical technology.

While most in the Church of God are no longer hostile toward medical science, neither should we depend on medical technology to stave off death. We may use the skills of doctors as gifts from God to help us through life. And we may approach death victoriously.

American evangelicalism,[19] on the other hand, presented the Terri Schiavo case as a clear-cut moral issue. *Christianity Today* treated it as one of the leading news stories of the day. James Dobson, of Focus on the Family, spoke as a leader among evangelicals, arguing that Terri should be kept alive. Numerous other evangelical voices chimed in, including Operation Rescue and the Christian Broadcasting Network.

Randall Terry, of Operation Rescue, presented himself as a spokesperson for Terri's parents. The headline of an article published by Operation Rescue on April 7, 2005, declared, "The Blood of Martyrs Is the Seed of Christians." An opening line referred to "the appalling state-sanctioned attempted murder of Terri Schiavo." This was typical of the hyperbole used by evangelical groups in speaking of the Schiavo case.

---

17. Teasley, "We'll Praise the Lord.".

18. Oldham, "Let Me See Jesus Only."

19. I am using *evangelical* in a restricted sense, as explained in the Introduction and Appendix B.

Troy Newman, president of Operation Rescue, used the Terri Schiavo case as an occasion for fund-raising.[20]

Focus on the Family disputed the report that Terri was comatose or in a persistive vegetative state. Instead, they presented her as a poster child for people with disability, saying that she merely suffered brain damage. The same article acknowledged, "There are times in the dying process when forced hydration via a feeding tube can be burdensome to the patient as the body is shutting down to die. In these situations, a feeding tube may be ethically removed with the concurrence of the guardian and/or family." They further acknowledged, "There is a time to die (Ecclesiastes 3:2), and therefore there are situations when medical interventions should cease and a natural death be allowed."[21] These acknowledgements were refreshing, yet they stood in contrast to the organization's blatant declarations that allowing Terri to die was immoral and a crime.

Biblical texts address this issue tangentially at best. The apostle Paul sees life in this world as a temporary matter that precedes a greater glory to come.

> Therefore we do not lose heart. Though outwardly we are wasting away, yet inwardly we are being renewed day by day...we fix our eyes not on what is seen, but on what is unseen. For what is seen is temporary, but what is unseen is eternal. Now we know that if the earthly tent we live in is destroyed, we have a building from God, an eternal house in heaven, not built by human hands...Therefore we are always confident and know that as long as we are at home in the body we are away from the Lord...We are confident, I say, and would prefer to be away from the body and at home with the Lord. (2 Cor 4:16, 18; 5:1, 6, 8)

---

20. Newman, "Blood of Martyrs."
21. Focus on the Family, "FOF Offers Insight."

For to me, to live is Christ and to die is gain. If I am to go on living in the body, this will mean fruitful labor for me. Yet what shall I choose? I do not know! I am torn between the two: I desire to depart and be with Christ, which is better by far; but it is more necessary for you that I remain in the body. (Phil 1:21–24)

In 2 Peter, we find a similar perspective: "I think it is right to refresh your memory as long as I live in the tent of this body, because I know that I will soon put it aside, as our Lord Jesus Christ has made clear to me" (2 Pet 1:13–14).

When discussing the matter of technology, death, and ethics, some Christians perceive the core issue as personhood: every person has infinite value and should be protected at all costs. "(Wesley) Smith points out that other bioethicists narrow protection further, requiring rationality, the capacity to experience desire, or the ability to value one's own existence."[22]

Some evangelicals overlook this fundamental issue: our attitude toward life and death itself. Is there nothing of greater value than life in this world? Must we oppose all death, as though death constitutes the great enemy? Have we nothing more to experience than this world? Does God expect us to use any means available to prolong physical life?

Persons of every age should think seriously about their wishes and express those wishes clearly, in writing. This is not just for persons over seventy. Remember, Terri Schiavo was a young woman when she lost consciousness. We should plan for the possibility that we will be incapacitated and our families will be similarly divided over what is best for us. The American Hospital Association has provided a Web site (www.putitinwriting.org) with legal forms and guidance for you.[23] Wisdom directs that you go beyond writing a Living Will to designate a "durable

---

22. Leo, "End of the Affair." This article provides a critique of the way both sides handled the Terri Schiavo case.

23. Austin, "AHA Sees Lots of Interest."

power of attorney for health care." In the event of incapacitation, this appears to be the strongest legal safeguard. The combination of a living will and a durable power of attorney for health care is known as an "advance directive." You should not assume that marriage provides your spouse with the authority to act as your medical surrogate or end-of-life proxy. A court may still name another guardian if you have not protected your rights, particularly if those closest to you differ in their opinions. Such a serious matter deserves consultation with a competent attorney immediately.

We must overcome the rational and emotional obstacles to making decisions about the use of medical technology at the end of life. Christians should be proclaiming the good news of eternal life, not compounding the pain of anxious families with our inadequate theology. Some evangelicals have used this issue to generate considerable publicity for themselves while alienating the people they are trying to help. Let us be agents of the grace of God, who will help people make responsible moral choices as they face death.

FOR FURTHER STUDY

Smith, Frederick G.. *What the Bible Teaches.* Anderson, IN: Gospel Trumpet Co,, 1914. 141–55

Byrum, Russell R. *Christian Theology.* Anderson, IN: Gospel Trumpet Co., 1925. See chap. 7, "Divine Physical Healing."

Strege, Merle D. *I Saw the Church.* Anderson, IN: Warner Press, 2002. See pp. 66–74, 232–34.

QUESTIONS FOR DISCUSSION

1. What does it mean to be pro-life? How do your values on life influence your position on the following?
   • Abortion
   • Use of life support technology
   • Euthanasia
   • Capital punishment

2. What are your wishes for use of life-support technology when you approach death? Have you completed the appropriate legal documents to record your wishes? Have you designated someone who has durable power of attorney for health care in the event that you are incapacitated?

3. Why do we Christians find it so difficult to discuss the issues surrounding death?

4. What does our response to death reveal about our theology?

5. How can you help people near you who are coping with difficult decisions regarding the impending death of someone they love?

8.

Can We All Get Along?

MARCIA COULD not believe what happened to her church. Three years ago, she and a handful of others had come together to launch a new congregation on the edge of the city. The church had been well funded and used the latest methods to reach unchurched people. They had found great success in attracting people, most of whom had not been involved in any church lately. In a short time, over 250 people were present for worship each Sunday.

Then a series of controversies wreaked havoc in the new congregation. One of the people who joined the congregation wanted to teach a series on the rapture and tribulation. Several expressed dissent because they thought the worship was not expressive enough and should incorporate opportunity for people to deliver words of prophecy. Another wanted to see the church take the lead in opposing same-sex marriage. Several families were lost when the leadership discovered that one of the small groups was teaching "once saved, always saved." When a new group leader was substituted, the entire group pulled out of the church. Several interrelated families were attracted to the church because they had been part of a Church of God congregation where they had previously lived. After attending several months, they became increasingly dissatisfied because the worship style was based on contemporary choruses and did not use the Church of God heritage songs they cherished. They finally dropped out as a group.

By the end, less than twenty-five people were attending services at the school building that the congregation had been renting. The pastor resigned in discouragement last month and took a job selling shoes at a nearby department store. Those who were left were so demoralized they could not continue the church plant. Marcia is not sure if she wants to be part of another church, and she certainly does not want anything to do with the Church of God.

The title for this chapter is taken from Rodney King, an African-American resident of Los Angeles. Early on the morning of March 3, 1991, King was beaten by police officers in plain view of a video camera. This set off a series of riots across Los Angeles. In response to the destructive violence, King made this poignant plea: "Can we all get along? Can we get along?" The question is pertinent to our discussion of theological change in the Church of God. How does this movement that has always treasured unity cope with diversity within its own ranks? Can we get along with people in our midst who have different beliefs, different values, and different traditions from ours?

To answer these questions, we need to understand how we are similar to other Christian groups—and how we are different. Central to the Church of God heritage are our convictions about holiness and unity. These convictions are similar to those of other church groups, while distinguishing us in their peculiar combination. Whereas all Christian traditions hold common beliefs about God's forgiveness of sins in the atonement, the Church of God is squarely within the Holiness tradition, which believes that the atonement includes a divine empowerment to live in victory over sin. Whereas some Christian traditions define Christian identity in terms of commonly held doctrines, the Church of God has always defined Christian identity in more experiential terms.

The ideals of Church of God heritage are well expressed in our songs. In the early days of this movement, the Church of God was understood to be a pure manifestation of the true church where all God's children could come together in unity. "Here every tribe and kindred come in fellowship so sweet."[1] The expectation of early Church of God leaders has been labeled "come-outism," because they exhorted other Christians to come out of Babylon (denominational churches). Our early leaders' dream of fostering a restoration of the New Testament church was expressed in the heritage song "The Reformation Glory":

---

1. Teasley, "Church of the Living God."

There's a mighty reformation sweeping o'er the land,
God is gathering His people by His mighty hand;
For the cloudy day is ending and the evening sun is bright,
With a shout of joy we hail the light.

When the voice from heaven sounded, warning all to flee
From the darksome courts of Babel back to Zion free;
Glad my heart to hear the message, and I hastened to obey,
And I'm standing in the truth today.

Zion's walls again are building as in days of yore,
And the scattered hosts returning to their land once more
Are rejoicing in their freedom, pledging evermore to stand
In the reformation truths so grand.

Christians all should dwell together in the bonds of peace,
All the clashing of opinion, all the strife should cease;
Let divisions be forsaken, all the holy join in one,
And the will of God in all be done.

O the reformation glory!
Let it shine to every land.
We will tell the blessed story;
In its truth we e'er shall stand.[2]

Some would consider this idealism to be naiveté, but it was the driv-
ing *raison d'etre* of the movement. In response to the message of holiness and unity, many Christians abandoned mainline denominations to
join the movement. This motif is also seen in the song that some have
described as the anthem of the Church of God:

The light of eventide now shines the darkness to dispel,
The glories of fair Zion's state ten thousand voices tell;
For out of Babel God doth call His scattered saints in one,
Together all one church compose, the body of His Son.

---

2. Naylor, "The Reformation Glory."

The Bible is our rule of faith and Christ alone is Lord,
All we are equal in His sight when we obey His Word;
No earthly master do we know, to Christ alone we bow,
And to each other and to God eternal trueness vow.

The day of sects and creeds for us forevermore is past,
God's unity joins all the saints upon the world so vast;
We reach our hands in fellowship to every blood-washed one,
While love entwines about each heart in which God's will is done.

O blessed truth that broke our bonds! In it we now rejoice,
While in the holy church of God we hear our Savior's voice;
And gladly to His blessed will submissive we shall be,
And from the yokes of Babel's lords from henceforth we are free.

O church of God, the day of jubilee
Has dawned so bright and glorious for thee;
Rejoice, be glad! The shepherd has begun
His long divided flock again to gather into one.[3]

Another song declares, "Never in sects to be scattered, Never again to do wrong; / Unity, holiness, heaven, Ever shall be our song."[4] The Church of God intended to be a pure church without division.

Likewise, the evangelical[5] movement of the last century had strong elements of antisectarianism. While maintaining the core beliefs of fundamentalism, evangelicals rejected the radical exclusivism that so characterized fundamentalists.[6] Fundamentalists tended to denounce and separate themselves from the surrounding culture. Evangelicals sought to take a gentler approach.

---

3. Naylor, "The Church's Jubilee."

4. Teasley, "Back to the Blessed Old Bible."

5. I am using *evangelical* in a restricted sense, as explained in the Introduction and Appendix B.

6. The five fundamentals were (1) the inerrancy of the Bible, (2) the virgin birth, (3) the substitutionary atonement, (4) the bodily resurrection of Jesus, and (5) and the second coming (premillenial). Evangelicals continue to hold these fundamentals (sometimes adapting one or more).

There is a certain overlap between fundamentalist and evangelical. Both are the conservative end of Protestantism. However in practice the term evangelical refers to a somewhat "softer" conservative approach. Evangelicals are more interested in working with other churches and more likely to become engaged with the culture. The Dictionary of Christianity in America says "Eventually, the term fundamentalist came to refer to militantly antimodernistic Protestant evangelicals in general."[7]

Evangelical is the self-ascribed label for a coalition that arose during the Second World War. This group came into being as a reaction against the perceived anti-intellectual separatist, belligerent nature of the fundamentalist movement in the 1920s and 1930s.[8]

Since the 1940s, the evangelical movement has grown in strength as the voice of conservative Christianity. The National Association of Evangelicals (NAE), in particular, is committed to Christian unity and cooperative ministry. While fundamentalism tends to be limited to churches of Reformed heritage, the NAE also includes churches from Pentecostal, Holiness, and Anabaptist traditions.

The modern evangelical movement still has a more strident element that continues the separatist heritage of the fundamentalist movement. Organizations like the Moral Majority and the Christian Coalition have exerted political influence upon national and state elections to promote the values of the Christian Right. James Dobson and his organization, Focus on the Family, evolved from a ministry devoted to teaching conservative family values to a political force addressing issues like homosexual rights. At the extreme conservative end, the Moral Reconstructionist movement seeks to remake the culture of the United States in the mold of Mosaic law. The Evangelical Theological Society (ETS)

---

7. "Where Did All Those Denominations Come From?"
8. Eskridge, "Defining Evangelicalism."

defines itself by the conviction that the Bible is inerrant. Some members of this organization, such as Dr. Clark Pinnock, have tried for decades to redefine inerrancy in a more moderate way, but they have been taken to task by the ETS.

While the Church of God was born in the same era as Fundamentalism, it pursued a markedly different path. As Strege observes, "The Church of God was never a very good candidate to join cause with Fundamentalism."[9]

> Fundamentalism also rested on a rationalist epistemology that seemed inevitably to insist on doctrinal statements as the foundation of fellowship. Indeed some Fundamentalists defined a Christian on the basis of whether he or she would subscribe to a list of "fundamentals." To insist on a creed or doctrinal statement as the basis of Christian fellowship violated one of the very deepest theological commitments of the Church of God movement."[10]

The Church of God shares common ground with evangelicals in the commitment to Christian unity. Although "come-outism" has been a theme of some leaders in our history, most have aspired to "reach our hands in fellowship to every blood-washed one." Since the middle of the twentieth century, evangelical groups such as the NAE have sought to do the same. In recent years, evangelical groups like Promise Keepers have provided avenues for Christians to come together across denominational and doctrinal lines.

While evangelicals have maintained the Fundamentalist practice of defining Christian identity in terms of a person's doctrinal stance, the Church of God has always believed that a person's Christian identity is defined solely by a personal relationship with Jesus Christ. Many in the Church of God hold beliefs close to, if not identical with, the five core beliefs of Fundamentalists:

---

9. Strege, *I Saw the Church*, 313.
10. Ibid.

- The divine inspiration and authority of the Bible,
- The incarnation and/or the virgin birth,
- Salvation through the blood of Jesus,
- The bodily resurrection of Jesus, and
- The second coming.

But the insistence on defining Christian identity as the acceptance of such a set of beliefs is creedalism, and creedalism has always been abhorrent to Church of God people.

In some ways, the Church of God has evolved in contrast to the development of evangelicalism. When evangelicals were fortifying themselves against liberalism, Church of God leaders were learning from them. These bridge-building leaders included Harold L. Phillips, T. Franklin Miller, Earl Martin, Adam Miller, Gene Newberry, Robert Reardon, John W. V. Smith, Irene Smith Caldwell, and Louis E. "Pete" Meyer. From 1930 on, Church of God scholars moved away from the church-historical interpretation of apocalyptic at the same time that evangelicals embraced more dispensational views. Although early Church of God evangelists preached a "come-out" message with respect to other Christian groups, later leaders such as Gene Newberry took a less caustic approach to other church traditions because they learned to appreciate their colleagues from those traditions. These leaders provide a model for us.[11]

Historian Strege says that the Church of God moved to the mainstream of American life from 1945 to 1970, while the evangelical movement was gaining power in the culture.[12] Also during this time of transition, an increasing number of Church of God laypersons identified with the values of evangelicalism. The result is that most grassroots Church of God people now identify themselves as conservative and suspect that their national leaders have fallen under the spell of liberalism.

In the 1960s and 1970s, the Church of God struggled to practice its ideals of Christian unity. Several issues threatened to polarize the

---

11. Ibid., 235–36, 244.
12. Ibid., 312.

movement into schism. Conversations had taken place between key leaders in the Church of God and representatives from other church groups, considering some form of closer cooperation or merger. Other leaders of the movement felt threatened by such overtures, sensing that they undermined the mission of the Church of God. The existence of an African-American version of the Church of God troubled some as inconsistent with our historic doctrine of unity. Efforts were made to include ethnic minorities in the highest levels of national church leadership. Also troubling for some was a decline in the number of women in leadership, both as pastors of local churches and as national leaders. Some prominent ministers advocated theological positions that struck others as liberal. Some groups leveled charges that our colleges were corrupting the theology of the church. While such differences in culture and theology threatened to divide the movement, some held that this very diversity made the Church of God strong.[13] In the words of theologian Gilbert Stafford:

> "Common mission and witness" does not require one way to conduct the life and work of the church at large. Rather, it calls for integrative compatibility of services, structures, and ministries. Some say unity means uniformity. They demand one way of serving God and others, one way to structure and govern the church, and one form of ministry for all. In order for the church to be in health, however, it needs a diversification of services, of structures, and of ministries.
>
> Monolithic sameness is not a sign of good health but of illness. Since the church is one in Christ, diversified services, structures, and ministries need to be compatible to the whole, and none competitive with the others; thus the term, integrative compatibility.[14]

---

13. Ibid., 317–48. Strege details tensions over race and gender, the Open Letter controversy of 1981, and the contributions of Adam Miller, John W. V. Smith, T. Franklin Miller, and James Earl Massey to the understanding of unity.

14. Stafford, *Theology for Disciples*, 239, 239–40.

The Church of God is certainly more heterogeneous today than it was in the early years. By practicing inclusiveness, we have incorporated people from other church backgrounds. These people inevitably bring with them beliefs that differ from those of our heritage. The challenges posed by these "immigrants" to the Church of God motivated the writing of this book. How are we to respond when people bring to the movement beliefs that conflict with our heritage? While these immigrants to the Church of God carry unwanted baggage, perhaps they also bring strengths. Our challenge is to identify what convictions are vital to our Christian heritage and what areas should remain open for discussion.

Gilbert Stafford offers guidelines for "Relating to Those Who Make Other Truth Claims." While Stafford enumerated these guidelines while addressing the need for dialogue with persons outside the Christian tradition, his concepts also apply to conversations with Christians from other church groups. Stafford offers six options, three of which assume we cannot know the truth, while the other three assume we can know the truth: casual interest, zealous dogmatism, dialogical search for truth, withdrawal, numerical triumphalism, dialogical engagement. Stafford commends the last option in particular. He believes we can engage in dialogue with others, confident that our understanding is rooted in truth, while remaining humbly open to the possibility that we can learn from their insights.[15]

Perhaps the most painful example of theological conflict in recent years has been over the doctrine of *glossalalia* (speaking in tongues). In some cases, individuals from Pentecostal traditions have entered Church of God congregations. In other cases, people already part of a Church of God congregation have had ecstatic experiences, usually as a result of participating in a charismatic worship event. The Church of God has generally not followed the charismatic tradition. In particular, the idea that speaking in tongues is the definitive mark of the baptism of the Holy Spirit is foreign to our Church of God heritage.

---

15. Ibid., 250–60.

Many Church of God persons find offensive other charismatic worship practices such as being slain in the Spirit and holy laughter.[16] Church of God congregations have been divided and even destroyed over this conflict. At the same time, some people and congregations in the movement have been more open to charismatic phenomena, particularly in the African-American community.

Another area of painful conflict is characterized by the labels *conservative* and *liberal*. We certainly have seen divergence of opinion among Church of God ministers on such theological issues, with an increasing polarization of theological convictions.

How are we to respond when others in the movement subscribe to beliefs that we would call liberal? Perhaps my brother accepts some conclusions of modern biblical scholarship with which I am not comfortable. Perhaps we differ over christology (the nature of Christ), soteriology (the nature of salvation) or the doctrine of sanctification. Perhaps my Christian co-worker believes that the theory of evolution provides a satisfactory explanation of our origins and is compatible with Christianity while I believe in creationism or intelligent design. Perhaps a woman in my Bible study believes that homosexuality is an acceptable lifestyle choice for Christians while I believe the Bible forbids such practices. There may be some people in my congregation who believe that abortion is a basic human right while I believe it is immoral.

Further, what am I to do when my brother is an evangelical? This book is written to address a drift of many of us toward the Christian Right. What if I have someone in my church who believes that inerrancy is a critical part of the doctrine of biblical inspiration? What do I do if someone in my Bible study is an avid reader of the Left Behind books? What if my pastor believes that God never calls women into ministry?

---

16. These practices are common among certain Pentecostals and charismatics. In the 1990s, the "Toronto Blessing" brought the practice of "holy laughter" or "the anointing of joy" to many churches. While these seem strange to many Church of God people today, Ken Tippen documented reports of similar occurrences in the early meetings of the Church of God!

Within the Church of God, some of us feel disturbed about changes within our own heritage. Many still subscribe to the apocalyptic teachings of the first generation—that Revelation provides predictions of world history and church development, leading to the founding of the Church of God—while others reject this interpretation of Scripture. Some have pacifist convictions while others believe that war is required at times. Some continue to lay hands on the sick and anoint them with oil, refusing to consult doctors or take medication, while others view medical science as a gift from God.

We still struggle to live our beliefs when it comes to race and culture. In recent years, the topic of racial reconciliation has received considerable attention. Within the Church of God, we have many African Americans and growing numbers of Hispanics, native Americans, and Asians. Many of us worship in congregations of blended ethnicity. At the same time, we have a number of congregations that primarily minister with persons of color. Among the largest Church of God congregations in the United States are those led and primarily comprised of ethnic minorities. What changes do we need to make so that we can practice what we preach about the unity of the church?

The Church of God is faced with the possibility of schism along several fault lines. We have African Americans who identify with the National Association and the annual camp meeting at West Middlesex. A growing Hispanic fellowship known as the Concilio has its own national meetings as well.

Not all of the possible fault lines are delineated by race or language. Many Church of God people west of the Rocky Mountains have long felt alienation from churches of the Midwest and the general offices in Anderson, Indiana. Some of our churches in various parts of the country use progressive styles of ministry that set them apart from our more traditional churches. Some newer congregations have upbeat worship services and sing praise choruses; other churches still sing the heritage songs in the hymnal and observe worship practices traditionally associated with the Church of God. Even our "traditional" congregations could divide into the ultraconservative wing and a more moderate traditional group. In a worst-case scenario, we might see six distinct denominations splinter from this movement that was founded in the name of unity.

How do we cope with all our differences? At the least, we must practice civility with each other and demonstrate Christian love above all of our disagreements. Many of the issues about which we disagree are truly minor issues, and should not come between us. Surely we can agree to disagree while we mutually strive to discern God's will.

Are some issues so significant that they should divide us? Does it matter if some believe the Bible is merely a compilation of ancient literature? Can we practice Christian unity while some among us question the deity of Jesus? Does it matter when a Church of God pastor denies the possibility of personal holiness? Is it acceptable for a Bible study to propagate end-time beliefs that are foreign to the Church of God? As important as Christian unity and tolerance are, other values may take precedence.

Semantics are significant. We cannot pretend that in using the same words, we all mean the same thing. Just because a person calls himself or herself a Christian does not mean he or she is one. On the other hand, just because a person disagrees with my beliefs, I cannot assume that person is not a Christian.

Throughout this book, I have attempted to contrast Church of God people with evangelical people. While these two groups of Christians have commonalities, they also have distinctive identities. Integrity demands that we be true to ourselves. While we must relate to all persons in Christian love, we should discern significant differences in our beliefs. While we may use the same terms, we may understand these terms in significantly different ways. Let us establish common ground with others wherever we can. Let us humbly and boldly proclaim truth as best we can. We do not need to demonize other Christians to be faithful to God and his church. Neither do we need to cower in silence when others misrepresent the teachings of Christianity. "God did not give us a spirit of timidity, but a spirit of power, of love and of self-discipline" (2 Tim 1:7).

Smith, John W. V. *I Will Build My Church: Biblical Insights on Distinguishing Doctrines of the Church of God.* Anderson, IN: Warner Press, 1985

Strege, Merle D. *I Saw the Church.* Anderson, IN: Warner Press, 2002.

Stafford, Gilbert W. *Theology for Disciples.* Anderson, IN: Warner Press, 1996.

Gray, Albert F. *Christian Theology.* Anderson, IN: Gospel Trumpet Company, 1946.

Byrum, Russell R. *Christian Theology.* Anderson, IN: Gospel Trumpet Company. 1925.

QUESTIONS FOR DISCUSSION

1. What do we mean when we sing, "We reach our hands in fellowship to every blood-washed one?"

2. How can we preach against denominationalism and not become another denomination ourselves?

3. Discuss the reasons why some in the Church of God have not identified completely with the fundamentalist or evangelical movements.

4. Discuss the issues that Dr. Hickson says threaten to divide our unity within the Church of God. Can you identify others?

5. Discuss the challenges presented to the Church of God by our inclusion of people from other church traditions.

6. Does it matter whether the Church of God holds onto its traditional beliefs? Where must we hold fast to our tradition, and where can we be flexible?

7. What do you recommend for future theological dialogues within the Church of God? With other church groups?

Appendix A

What Is the Church of God?

EVEN THOUGH I have written this book to people of the Church of God, I expect that many of my readers will not be familiar with the richness of our Church of God heritage. Old-timers are chagrined because many of our congregations do not even carry the name Church of God emblazoned on their signs.[1] People in these churches may not have attended camp meetings at the national or regional level. So I offer this brief explanation to round out the reader's understanding of what the Church of God is.

The Church of God movement traces its history to 1881. What happened then was a convergence of the Holiness Movement and nondenominational trends in American Christianity. The holiness movement included people from Methodism and others who followed the teaching of John Wesley, as well as American evangelists like Charles Finney. Thomas and Alexander Campbell and others spoke a rising voice against sectarianism. The people who came out to the Church of God tended to come from Wesleyan or Anabaptist traditions.

So we find three major streams combining in Church of God heritage: nondenominational, holiness, and free church.[2] The Church of God shares the Wesleyan/holiness tradition with the Nazarenes, the Wesleyan Church in America, and the Free Methodists. The Church of God shares the antidenominational tradition with Christian Churches. The Church of God shares the Anabaptist tradition with the Menno-

---

1. I am not among those who think this is an issue. What matters to me is what is preached in the pulpit.

2. Free church as opposed to the state churches of Europe. Free churches tend to place church authority at the congregational level and tend to use a less formal style of worship.

nites, the Brethren, and Quakers. While the Church of God has much in common with Baptist churches, the two groups have distinctly different theological backgrounds: most Baptist churches are Calvinist. While the Church of God shares many of the values of evangelicalism, they are not the same: Evangelicals focus on right doctrine, but the Church of God focuses on right experience. The Church of God has never been as interested in ritual or right belief as in a vital relationship with God.

In the beginning, Church of God people had no intention of starting a new denomination. The whole idea was that denominations are evil; Christians should not be divided. The message of the Church of God was to "come out" from "Babylon" to the true church.[3] The focal point originally was not a group of churches but a Christian newspaper that was distributed widely; people found the Church of God by reading the *Gospel Trumpet*. Over time, congregations evolved from reading the paper or hearing a traveling preacher. In the early years, the *Gospel Trumpet* discouraged ministers from settling down. These traveling preachers were known as flying messengers. Since the end of time was expected soon, the preachers' imperative was to proclaim the gospel as widely as possible.

Over decades, local churches began to develop and we established national organizations that are typical of denominations. The first was a Missionary Committee, seeking to coordinate the work of flying messengers who went beyond the United States. Colleges sprang up in several places.[4] A Board of Church Extension and Home Missions was established to coordinate the work within the United States in places where the Church of God was weak, especially in the larger cities. A Board of Christian Education was established to assist congregations with this ministry. Beginning in 1917, a General Ministerial Assembly convened in Anderson to discuss issues of common concern. This is now know as the General Assembly and includes lay representation

---

3. The title of Babylon was taken from the book of Revelation and used in reference to denominational Christianity.

4. See chapter 5 for information on the development of Church of God colleges.

from congregations and area ministries. In the 1990s, our polity was restructured so that ministry in the United States is incorporated under Church of God Ministries, Inc., and most of the national agencies were included in this structure. The *Yearbook of the Church of God* provides a registry for congregations and pastors recognized by the Church of God. For some time now, it has been apparent that the Church of God has developed all of the organizational marks of a denomination. Yet we continue to hold to the aspirations of unity that gave us birth.

The Church of God shares the core beliefs common to all Christian traditions, whether modern American evangelicals or Christians of the ages. These beliefs include the doctrine of God, man, sin, Christ, and salvation.

Some Church of God beliefs are held in common with mainline Protestants. We believe in justification by faith (that we are forgiven of sin through the death of Jesus Christ on the cross). We value the priesthood of all believers (that every Christian has direct access to God and is called to represent God to the world). We believe that the Bible is the sole basis of authority for doctrine, as opposed to trusting the teachings of an apostolic succession of bishops. These beliefs we share with all Christians whose tradition is rooted in the Protestant Reformation, whether Lutheran, Reformed, or Anglican.

The Church of God has much in common with Christians whose tradition is rooted in the Radical Reformation, who are also known as Anabaptists. This group has been called the third wave of the Reformation in contrast with the Lutherans and Reformed Christians. Other church groups who descended from this part of the Reformation include Mennonites and Quakers. A distinctive practice of this group is believer's baptism as opposed to infant baptism (which is practiced by the Roman Catholic, Lutheran, and Reformed churches). Lutheran and Reformed churches were usually state churches, but the Anabaptists have insisted upon the separation of church and state. This conviction later influenced the political philosophy behind the founding of the United States. Anabaptist tradition is especially distinguished by its commitment to pacifism or nonviolence.

Christians from the Anabaptist tradition tend to hold ideals of restoring church life to the pattern of the New Testament Church, an idea that is also taught by the various Christian Church denominations. Whereas the Church of God has often called itself a reformation movement, the Christian Churches call themselves a restoration movement. (Our commonalities go beyond our rhyming titles, however.)

The Church of God has much in common with other Christian groups that grew out of the Holiness Movement. We tend to be Arminian in our theology rather than Calvinist: we emphasize the free will and moral accountability of persons more than the sovereignty of God. Holiness Churches draw many of their teachings from John Wesley, the eighteenth-century reformer of Anglican Christianity, whose followers became the Methodist Church. Like others of this tradition, we expect that a person's Christian faith results in changes of lifestyle and behavior. Where some Christians are excessively individualistic, we believe that the church has a responsibility for social reform.[5]

Two key beliefs are brought together by the Church of God more effectively than many Holiness groups have done: the belief in Christian unity and personal holiness. Our belief in unity holds that all Christians are part of one church and should not be divided by creed or denominational label. Our belief in holiness holds that Christians are empowered by the Holy Sprit to live in victory over sin. Neither of these beliefs are unique to the Church of God. What is notable is the way in which these two ideals come together to provide the core of Church of God heritage.

The first generation of the Church of God movement took offense at the sectarian spirit they found among the denominations of their day. They were convinced that God has only one church, made up of all who are in Christ. A similar attitude has since appeared elsewhere, particularly in the ecumenical movement and in evangelicalism.[6] But

---

5. John W. V. Smith, *I Will Build My Church*, 47–59.

6. This author is among those who saw in Promise Keepers a contemporary expression of Church of God idealism.

while it is popular these days to be nondenominational, the Church of God has always been *anti*denominational. Church of God pioneers were convinced that denominationalism was evil because it divides the people whom Christ made one. This is the root of our practice of disavowing church membership. We believe that the only membership book that matters is "the Lamb's Book of Life" (Rev 20:12). Another church group that originated in the nineteenth century with a similar commitment to Christian unity is the Christian Churches / Church of Christ.

The Church of God commitment to unity has been expressed in several catch phrases, some of which were part of the lyrics of our heritage songs. We assert, "We have no creed but the Bible," to express our desire to base our beliefs on nothing other than God's Word. We sing, "We reach our hands in fellowship to every blood-washed one," to affirm our open-door policy to all who know Jesus. Many of our church signs carry the slogan, "Where Christian experience makes you a member." Our personal testimonies have often included the declaration "I saw the church!" This describes the discovery of the universal bond that ties all Christians together.

Our commitment to Christian unity has manifested itself in several ways. We tend to be more interested in experiential commonality than doctrinal conformity. The question we care about is not, Do you believe these things? but, Do you know Jesus? This experiential approach to faith is one of the most significant differences between the Church of God and evangelicalism, which emphasizes doctrinal propositions.

For some, the name of the church is a critical issue. Any name other than Church of God is seen as an act of denominationalism and a betrayal of our principles. The doctrine of the church (ecclesiology) was a major theme of early Church of God preachers. They declared that the church is more than a human organization: It is a divine institution, founded and governed by the Holy Spirit. For this reason, the Church of God has long wrestled with the issue of proper organization and accountability. C. E. Brown, the fourth editor of the *Gospel Trumpet*, attempted to resolve the tension by saying, "We cannot organize the Church, but we must organize the work of the Church."[7]

A common theme (at least during the first fifty years of the movement) was "come-outism," the principle that Christians should break their affiliation with denominations to be part of the pure church. Over the years, this emphasis has waned. Most of us now see that the movement is prone to behave as much like a denomination as any other group.

While the most popular Church of God songs focus on the themes of Christian unity and experience, the theme of personal holiness drove Warner and others to compose memorable lyrics as well:

I ought to love my Savior; He pardoned all my sin,
Then sanctified my nature, And keeps me pure within.[8]

Fill me with Thy Spirit, Lord, Fully save my longing soul;
Thru the precious cleansing blood, Purify and make me whole.

Fill me with Thy holy light, I would have a single eye;
Make me perfect in Thy sight, 'Tis Thy will to sanctify.[9]

Lord, I would be wholly Thine, I would do Thy will divine,
From the world and sin and self I would be free:
On the altar now I lie, and with all my heart I cry,
Let the holy fire from heaven fall on me.

I would have sufficient grace every foe to bravely face,
And an overcomer evermore to be;
That I well may fill my place, and that I might win the race,
Let the holy fire from heaven fall on me.

Holy Spirit from above, fill my longing soul with love,
Till the Master's image all in me may see;

---

7. John W. V. Smith, *Quest for Holiness and Unity*, 318.

8. Warner, "I Ought to Love My Savior."

9. Warner, "Fill Me with Thy Spirit, Lord."

Make me gentle, true and kind, meek of heart and humble mind,
Let the holy fire from heaven fall on me.[10]

Note that this understanding of holiness is based on a particular understanding of sin. We tend to prefer a more limited definition of sin: sin is willful transgression. Sanctification is seen as a change of heart so that we no longer choose to live in disobedience to God. John W.V. Smith said, "Living a life completely under the direction of the Holy Sprit means living with victory over sinful desires and temptations."[11] One of the biblical bases for this understanding of holiness comes from the apostle Paul:

> For the grace of God that brings salvation has appeared to all
> men. It teaches us to say "No" to ungodliness and worldly
> passions, and to live self-controlled, upright and godly lives
> in this present age, while we wait for the blessed hope—the
> glorious appearing of our great God and Savior, Jesus Christ,
> who gave himself for us to redeem us from all wickedness
> and to purify for himself a people that are his very own, eager to do what is good. (Titus 2:11–14)

Secondary to the emphases on unity and holiness, the Church of God heritage has included distinctive beliefs and practices about ordinances, divine healing, eschatology, and racial reconciliation. These will be discussed here. (Additional doctrinal distinctives —such as women in ministry, an amillennial eschatology and an Anabaptist commitment to peace—are discussed elsewhere in this book.[12]

The Church of God is one of the Christian traditions that prefer the term *ordinance* over *sacrament*.[13] Most Protestant churches have nar-

---

10. Henry, "Let the Fire Fall on Me."

11. John W. V. Smith, *I Will Build My Church*, 85.

12. Chapter 3 discusses the contrast in teachings about end times between evangelicals and the Church of God. Chapter 4 addresses ordination of women to ministry. Chapter 6 describes the influence of the Anabaptist tradition on our view of politics, patriotism, and pacifism.

13. John W. V. Smith, *I Will Build My Church*, 117–32.

rowed the list of sacraments to two: baptism and Communion.[14] By not calling these sacraments, the Church of God is denying that these are means of communicating God's grace; rather we call them ordinances because we are following these worship practices in obedience to God's command.[15]

In addition to baptism and Communion, the Church of God has long practiced footwashing as an ordinance. This practice is taken from John 13 where Jesus said that we should wash one another's feet as he modeled. Many Christians see this language as only figurative of the command to serve. The Church of God has taken this more literally, counting footwashing as an ordinance along with baptism and Communion.[16] Most see footwashing simply as an act of humility, but the power of footwashing as a symbol is found in its expression of community. In modern times, this practice only takes place within the family of God: the one who washes my feet is truly my brother. This expression of community is often followed by a hug. While one cannot deny the message of humility, it is the message of community that makes footwashing a cherished practice.

In the Church of God, we teach that baptism is a profession of faith for believers only (not infants) and should be performed by immersion. Baptism represents (1) spiritual cleansing, (2) dying with Christ, and (3) being resurrected with Christ.

The ordinance of Communion serves as a memorial of the Last Supper and the Passion that followed. In Communion, we engage in an act of worship and thanksgiving. We proclaim the power of Christ's sacrifice until he returns. Communion provides a testimony of unity: a horizontal act of fellowship with all who belong to Christ. In contrast to some other Christian groups, the Church of God rejects the idea

---

14. Classic Roman Catholic doctrine holds that there are seven sacraments: baptism, confirmation, Eucharist, penance, matrimony, ordination, and unction (prayer for the sick).

15. Since God has ordained that we do these, we call them ordinances.

16. In truth, few in the Church of God would hold footwashing on the same level as the other two ordinances.

that we recrucify Christ in taking Communion or that there is value to taking Communion apart from faith. The Church of God celebrates an open table, which means that all Christian believers are welcome to partake, whether or not they identify with a Church of God congregation. The Church of God generally does not require that the person presiding at a Communion service be ordained. Most Church of God congregations observe the ordinances on a comparatively infrequent basis, though some congregations will celebrate Communion once a month. Baptism is observed only when a person makes a profession of faith in Christ. Footwashing may be performed once a year, often on the Thursday before Easter.[17]

The Church of God has historically believed in divine healing.[18] This belief was much more dominant in our first quarter-century under the leadership of E. E. Byrum. Camp-meeting services have routinely included a time of anointing and prayer for the sick. Displays of crutches and other medical paraphernalia that were no longer needed by persons who had been healed could be found in the early offices of *Gospel Trumpet*. At times, the belief in divine healing was so strong that medical doctors were not consulted and pharmaceuticals were not used. Some correction was forced by the presence of sickness, disability, and death among indisputably godly people, particularly in the debilitating injury of C. W. Naylor and the tragic death of the children of Clarence and Nora Hunter.[19] Another factor that cooled our passion in the area of divine healing was our reaction against extreme teachings among Pentecostals. For Church of God people (especially as taught by E. E. Byrum), the foundation of the doctrine of divine healing was the conviction that sickness is a consequence of sin and that the salvation purchased by Christ's death on the cross includes liberation from disease. Many in the Church of God today would question this.

---

17. This is known as Maundy Thursday, a part of Holy Week. Tradition holds that this was the night that Jesus shared the Last Supper with his disciples where he washed their feet.

18. John W. V. Smith, *I Will Build My Church*, 133–47.

19. Strege, *I Saw the Church*, 232–34.

A key verse for our practice of praying for divine healing is James 5:14, "Is any one of you sick? He should call the elders of the church to pray over him and anoint him with oil in the name of the Lord." After quoting this verse, Church of God people will often anoint sick people with oil, lay hands on them, and pray corporately. Divine healing is not emphasized as much today as in the earliest decades of the movement, but camp meetings still devote at least one worship service to prayer for divine healing, and most congregations extend altar calls at the end of their worship services, anointing the sick who come for prayer.

The Church of God has from the earliest days included people of different races or ethnicities. To some extent, this is a natural result of our commitment to Christ's teaching about the unity of all Christians. To our shame, we have not always lived out our ideals. At the zenith of the Ku Klux Klan, we often yielded to social pressure and segregated our worship services. In response, blacks in the Church of God formed their own fellowship with its own meetings, centered in West Middlesex, Pennsylvania. In recent years, the Church of God has worked to affect racial reconciliation at all levels. Black leaders hold positions of national leadership. A survey of the *Yearbook of the Church of God* shows that our largest congregations are led by black pastors and are comprised predominately of black laypeople.

The Church of God has grown from a scattering of *Gospel Trumpet* subscribers to a global fellowship. According to the *2005 Yearbook of the Church of God*, we have 2,240 congregations in the United States with 248,630 persons in worship services on an average Sunday morning. In the United States and Canada, the Church of God has over 5,124 ordained pastors. The work of the Church of God is spread across six continents. The Church of God has 7,148 congregations worldwide with 788,741 believers.[20]

Like nondenominational or Baptist churches, Church of God congregations are locally autonomous. We have no bishops or other external authorities over the local church. Even the General Assembly

---

20. Church of God Ministries, *2005 Yearbook*, 357, 359, 554.

that meets annually in Anderson, Indiana, exercises no ecclesiastical authority over the congregations of the Church of God. As we have long said, the Assembly speaks *to* the Church, not *for* the Church. Each congregation selects its own pastoral leadership by majority vote. We do not practice a formal membership: we believe that anyone who testifies to a salvation experience and participates in the life of the congregation is part of the church family.

This book discusses the contrasts between the Church of God and modern American evangelicalism, yet we have much in common. Both groups have the spirit of a movement. While the Church of God has evolved into an organization with denominational characteristics, evangelicalism continues to function as a movement. Many evangelicals identify more strongly with this movement than with whatever denomination they claim. Both groups developed in the American culture in response to elements of indigenous Christianity that they found to be unbiblical. Persons from both groups tend to be conservative in theology, lifestyle, and politics. These common features can obscure the distinctive beliefs that set the Church of God apart from most evangelicals.

FOR FURTHER STUDY

Callen, Barry L. *What We Teach*. Anderson, IN: Anderson University Press, 2005.

Smith, John W.V. *I Will Build My Church: Biblical Insights on Distinguishing Doctrines of the Church of God*. Anderson, IN: Warner Press, 1985.

Stafford, Gilbert W. *Theology for Disciples*. Anderson, IN: Warner Press, 1996.

Withrow, Oral, and Laura Withrow. *Meet Us at the Cross: An Introduction to the Church of God*. Anderson, IN: Warner Press, 1999.

Appendix B

What Is an Evangelical?

THROUGHOUT THIS book, I make reference to evangelicals, evangelical faith, and evangelicalism. This raises the question, What is an *evangelical?* Some believe that the Church of God is a part of evangelical Christianity. Plenty of Church of God people count themselves as evangelical, yet this book repeatedly contrasts evangelicalism with our Church of God heritage. How are they different?[1]

For some, the word *evangelical* carries a broad connotation. They may understand it to be so broad as to encompass all Christians; more likely, even those with a broad understanding of evangelicalism would say that it excludes people of the Roman Catholic or Eastern Orthodox traditions and includes only those of the Protestant tradition. The title of Helmut Thielicke's magnum opus, *The Evangelical Faith,* is one example of this broad definition of *evangelical.* Using this definition, the Church of God is surely a part of the evangelical world.

For some, the word *evangelical* implies the adoption of certain core beliefs. In this somewhat narrower definition, an *evangelical* is one who believes in Jesus Christ as God in flesh who gave his life for the salvation of sinners. Such people tend to see a direct connection between the words *evangelical* and *evangelism* and they would say that an evangelical Christian is one who values the transmission of the gospel to people who are lost. If *evangelical* means a Christian who takes the Bible seriously, who believes that Jesus is Lord and that Jesus died for the sins of the world and that the mission of the church is to proclaim that gospel

---

1. Evangelical theologian Stanley Grenz offers a very similar discussion of the definition of *evangelical* in *Revisioning Evangelical Theology,* 22–35.

to the world, then the Church of God certainly still conforms to this definition.

For the purposes of this book, I have limited the definition of *evangelical* to a more distinct group of persons and groups within the Christian faith. Generally, evangelicals ascribe to a Reformed theology, with its emphasis on the sovereignty of God and its rejection of Arminian teaching of human free will.[2] To the degree that evangelicals identify with Reformed theology, they exclude persons from the Church of God and other Wesleyan/Holiness traditions, such as is the Church of the Nazarene, the Free Methodist Church, and the Wesleyan Church in America.

Within the scope of this definition, *evangelicals* are Christians who espouse the five fundamentals originally formulated by the Fundamentalists, who preceded them: (1) the inerrancy of the Bible, (2) the virgin birth, (3) the substitutionary atonement of Christ, (4) the bodily resurrection of Jesus, and (5) the second coming of Christ before a thousand-year reign on earth (premillennial eschatology). While fundamentalists and evangelicals agree on these basic doctrines, evangelicals try to distinguish themselves with a less sectarian spirit and a willingness to engage with the culture around them.

Generally, Church of God persons have affirmed the intent of the five fundamentals but have understood them in different ways. As detailed in this book, the Church of God has not shared the evangelical passion for inerrancy. We have a very different understanding of eschatology than most evangelicals. So while Church of God heritage has much in common with the evangelical tradition, we do not fully conform to this narrow connotation of the word.

While most evangelicals would be uncomfortable with the label *fundamentalist*, the evangelical movement is a child of the older Fundamentalist movement. Fundamentalism was a reaction against the drift of mainline denominations toward liberal theology and German Biblical criticism. Key leaders were Carl McIntire, Bob Jones, and John R. Rice.

---

2. If this is unfamiliar, I discuss the matter at length in chapter 2.

During the 1920s, Fundamentalists worked on three key campaigns: (1) regaining control of Protestant denominations, mission boards, and seminaries; (2) supporting Prohibition, Sunday "blue laws," etc.; and (3) opposing the teaching of evolution in the public schools.

The Scopes trial discredited Fundamentalism in the minds of many in the United States. Fundamentalism came to be seen as shrill and extremist. One example of a fundamentalist school is Bob Jones University. One example of a fundamentalist publication is *The Sword of the Lord*. As this periodical's masthead declares, separatism is a key element in fundamentalism .As the Web site for evangelical Wheaton College says, "Since the 1940s, the term *fundamentalist* has come to denote a particularly aggressive style related to the conviction that the separation from cultural decadence and apostate (read *liberal*) churches are telling marks of faithfulness to Christ."[3] This abhorrence of separatism provided a key rationale for the development of evangelicalism in the 1940s.

> There is a certain overlap between fundamentalist and evangelical. Both are the conservative end of Protestantism. However in practice the term evangelical refers to a somewhat "softer" conservative approach. Evangelicals are more interested in working with other churches and more likely to become engaged with the culture. The *Dictionary of Christianity in America* says, "Eventually, the term fundamentalist came to refer to militantly antimodernistic Protestant evangelicals in general."[4]

With the decline of fundamentalism as a force in American religion, a number of individuals saw the need for a new movement of conservative Christians. The earliest leaders of modern evangelicalism included J. Elwin Wright, Harold John Ockenga, and Charles Fuller. The best-known evangelical leader is Billy Graham. Among leading

---

3. Eskridge, "Defining Evangelicalism."
4. Soc.Religion.Christianity. "Where Did All Those."

evangelical colleges are Moody Bible Institute and Wheaton College. Key evangelical organizations are the National Association of Evangelicals (NAE) and Youth for Christ. Wheaton's Web site further says, "Evangelical is the self-ascribed label for a coalition that arose during the Second World War. This group came into being as a reaction against the perceived anti-intellectual separatist, belligerent nature of the fundamentalist movement in the 1920s and 1930s."[5]

Where fundamentalists were stridently separatist, evangelicals strive to maintain a softer tone. In particular, the National Association of Evangelicals is committed to Christian unity and cooperative ministry. This group was established in 1942 and presents a Statement of Faith that is markedly moderate. Fundamentalism tended to be limited to churches of Reformed heritage, but the NAE has welcomed to its ranks the leaders of many church groups similar to the Church of God. .

> Whereas the fundamentalist movement that prefigured NAE was largely the domain of Baptists, Congregationalists, and Presbyterians in the northern part of the United States, NAE from the 1942 conference on, embraced numerous Christians in the Pentecostal, Holiness, and Anabaptist traditions. Pentecostalism, which had been kept at arm's length by most fundamentalists, had become part of the conservative alliance.[6]

Several national leaders of the Church of God, including former Executive-Secretary Edward L. Foggs, Sr., have participated in NAE activities.

An organization that fits the more restricted definition of *evangelical* is the Evangelical Theological Society (ETS). This organization has been a watchdog for conservative Christian theology, particularly of a Reformed tradition, since 1949. Under the title, "Doctrinal Basis," the ETS Web site offers this requirement for membership:

---

5. Eskridge, "Defining Evangelicalism."

6. National Association of Evangelicals. "History of the NAE."

The following doctrinal basis must be subscribed to by all members annually with the renewal of their membership in the Society.

"The Bible alone, and the Bible in its entirety, is the Word of God written and is therefore inerrant in the autographs. God is a Trinity, Father, Son, and Holy Spirit, each an uncreated person, one in essence, equal in power and glory."

Elsewhere on their Web site, ETS offers this definition: "We are, first of all, *Evangelical*—that is, we subscribe to the Good News of Salvation as a free gift of God through the sacrificial death of Jesus Christ on the cross."[7]

In the last two decades of the twentieth century, evangelicals who engaged in political activism in alliance with the Republican Party gained the label "the Christian Right." Leading this development was Christian Coalition, founded by television evangelist Pat Robertson. Earlier, Jerry Falwell's Moral Majority played a similar role. While the Christian Right played a role in the 1976 presidential election, they were disappointed by the Carter Administration's lack of response for their agenda. Still, several news commentators christened 1976 "The Year of the Evangelical."[8] The 1980 election provided a very different outcome, with the Reagan administration actively courting the Christian Right. While Reagan was hardly a model evangelical in terms of his sporadic church attendance, his political agenda endeared him to conservative Christians. The George H. W. Bush Administration continued the Republican relationship with the Christian Right, though not as closely. Evangelicals tended to be alienated by the politics of Bill Clinton in spite of his Baptist church membership, and they were appalled by the scandal dubbed "Monicagate." In 2000, evangelicals again found an occupant in the White House who actively courted their support.

---

7. http://www.etsjets.org/; accessed November 15, 2005.

8. "1976: 'The Year of the Evangelical,'" 1165. Attributions have also been made to *Time* and *Newsweek*.

Since the early 1970s, a leading cause among evangelicals has been abortion. Most evangelicals (as narrowly defined) are opposed to abortion on demand. An extreme expression of this conviction is Operation Rescue, which engages in protest activities even to the point of arrest. Some evangelicals shrink from such confrontational efforts, but participate in Crisis Pregnancy Centers or political lobbying to restrict access to abortion. One political goal of evangelicals is appointing justices to the Supreme Court who will overturn the *Roe v. Wade* abortion decision.

Most modern evangelicals share a set of beliefs about the last days described as dispensational premillennialism.[9] This set of doctrines originated in the early nineteenth century and gained popularity through Bible conferences promoted by well-known evangelists such as Dwight L. Moody. Evangelicals took comfort from the birth of the State of Israel in 1948, seeing this as a harbinger of prophecies soon to be fulfilled. In the 1970s, popular interest was again stirred with the publication of Hal Lindsay's *Late Great Planet Earth*. Nothing grabbed the interest of the masses quite like the Left Behind series of books and movies in the 1990s. Many evangelicals were swept up in the Y2K frenzy with expectations that the second millennium would end with the rapture. In spite of a series of false predictions, most evangelicals have not lost faith in so-called prophecy experts.

As was the case with fundamentalists, evolution continues to be a galvanizing issue for evangelicals. Since the writing of John Whitcomb and Henry Morris,[10] many evangelicals have encouraged the teaching of Creationism to challenge Darwin's theory of evolution. While the fundamentalists of the 1920s sought to penalize teachers for teaching evolution, today's evangelicals petition school boards to teach creationism (or intelligent design) as an alternative in science classes.

Some of the greatest leaders among conservative Christianity in the twentieth and twenty-first centuries have been evangelicals. Billy Gra-

---

9. This approach to eschatology is discussed in chapter 3.

10. Whitcomb and Morris, *Genesis Flood*.

ham is arguably the quintessential evangelical. Richard J. Foster notes that a rift developed between Graham and key fundamentalists in the 1950s because Graham sought to work in the most ecumenical settings available.[11] Nevertheless, his reputation grew and spanned denominational lines. Child psychologist James Dobson became another influential evangelical. Ironically, Dobson's background is with the Church of the Nazarene, a holiness denomination. But Dobson's political activism and opposition to homosexual rights has endeared him to the Christian Right. Chuck Colson began his career as a nonreligious political operative until his involvement in Watergate landed him in prison. While there, Colson experienced a conversion to Christ and founded Prison Fellowship, a ministry to prisoners and their families. Colson has also been vocal in commenting on social issues from an evangelical perspective. Pat Robertson came from a charismatic background to become a key player in evangelicalism, first through his Christian Broadcasting Network and later as a presidential candidate for the Republican Party.

Francis Schaeffer provided a philosophical apologetic for evangelicals. D. James Kennedy, pastor of Coral Ridge Presbyterian Church and founder of Evangelism Explosion, is one of many pastors who have developed a national standing as evangelical leaders. Tim LaHaye came from a career of writing books on marriage and temperament to writing a best-selling series of books and movies depicting Revelation from a premillennial perspective. Theologian Clark H. Pinnock provided an alternative approach to inerrancy until he was reined in by the Evangelical Theological Society.

The definition of *evangelical* used in this book agrees with the description given by Richard Foster. For Foster, the key attribute of evangelicals is a commitment to the Bible as the Word of God. Evangelicals are convinced that the Bible is "the only infallible rule of faith and practice."[12] For evangelicals, the authority of Scripture rises above

---

11. Foster, *Streams of Living Water*, 214.

12. Ibid., 222.

church tradition or personal experience. With the great reformers, the evangelical stands on *Sola Scriptura*. They also tend to affirm the classic statements of Christian faith, known as creeds. Evangelicals emphasize evangelism as the central mission of the church. For evangelicals, pure doctrine is of paramount importance. In the process of safeguarding doctrine, evangelicals can make majors out of minors: end times, inerrancy, women in ministry, and miracles.

Evangelicals tend to have a limited view of the salvation offered in Jesus. They seem to believe that the gospel promises nothing more than saving souls from eternal damnation. They would not agree with the understanding of other Protestants, Eastern Orthodox, or Roman Catholic Christians that biblical salvation is personal, social, and institutional.

The greatest weakness of evangelicals grows out of their greatest strength: their devotion to the Bible can become bibliolatry. This is why evangelicals tend to describe their doctrine of biblical inspiration with the word *inerrancy*. Evangelical artists sometimes use the image of Christ extending to us an open Bible, when the reality is that the Bible presents Christ to us. This symbol reveals a confusion of spiritual authority. As evangelical theologian Donald Bloesch says,

> The ultimate, final authority is not Scripture but the living God himself as we find him in Jesus Christ. Jesus Christ and the message about him constitute the material norm for our faith just as the Bible is the formal norm. The Bible is authoritative because it points beyond itself to the absolute authority, the living and transcendent Word of God.[13]

Foster believes that evangelicals need to return to the classic Christian formulation of *Christus Rex et Dominus Scripturae* (Christ is King and Lord of Scripture). Foster asserts, "Salvation is not in the Book but in Jesus Christ."[14] While the Bible is clearly authoritative for Christians, evangelicals have emphasized this to extreme.

---

13. Bloesch, *Essentials of Evangelical Theology*, 1:62–63.

14. Foster, *Streams of Living Water*, 231.

Some evangelicals have taken a more progressive path. They are rethinking some of the most basic elements of the evangelical tradition. Even propositional theology is under question in ways that resonate with our Church of God heritage. Some evangelicals are working to bridge the theological gulf between Calvinists and other traditions. Some are dramatically altering dispensationalism without abandoning this theory entirely. Some are expressing an openness to allowing women to serve in pastoral ministry. Some are creatively engaging the questions of postmodernity.

Stanley Grenz is one of the leading theologians of these progressive evangelicals.[15] Robert Webber has chronicled the work of the more progressive evangelical movement.[16] Even President Jimmy Carter has written a book protesting the right-wing extremism of his own Southern Baptist denomination.[17] In significant places, we can see that evangelicals are not what they used to be.

While this book largely counters evangelicalism as antithetical to the Church of God's heritage, these two groups have much in common. We share a strong commitment to the Bible as the uniquely inspired Word of God. We share an orthodox christology, believing Jesus to be God the Son who lived among us and give his life for the sins of the world. We believe that evangelism (sharing the gospel) is central to the mission of the church. We generally share conservative social and political philosophies. Most evangelicals have a congregational polity (church structure and government) not unlike the Church of God. Both movements are less than 150 years old, yet aspire to communicate New Testament Christianity as they understand it. At times, the most progressive evangelical thinkers seem to be moving in the same direction as the Church of God. Many people from a Church of God background have moved to evangelical churches with little discomfort and others in Church of God congregations hold decidedly evangelical convictions.

---

15. Grenz, *Revisioning Evangelical Theology*.

16. Webber, *Younger Evangelicals*.

17. Carter, *Our Endangered Values*.

I hope we can make the most of the similarities between the Church of God and evangelicalism while proclaiming the distinctive beliefs and values that set the Church of God apart.

FOR FURTHER STUDY

Grenz, Stanley. *Revisioning Evangelical Theology: A Fresh Agenda for the 21st Century*. Downers Grove, IL: InterVarsity Press, 1993.

Webber, Robert. *The Younger Evangelicals*. Grand Rapids, MI: Baker Books, 2002.

Bibliography

"1976: 'The Year of the Evangelical.'" *Christian Century*, December 29, 1976.

Albright, John. "Adam Was a Pacifist: Memorials to Peacemakers on AU Campus." *Church of God Peace Fellowship*, Summer 2005, 4. http://www.peacecog.com/newsletter/PF%20Summer%202005.pdf.

Armstrong, Chris. "Not a Mercy but a Sin." *CH Newsletter*, October 31, 2003. http://www.christianitytoday.com/history/newsletter/2003/oct31.html.

Austin, Kate. "AHA Sees Lots of Interest in Advance Directives Web Site." *AHA News*, May 16, 2005, 5.

Bloesch, Donald. *Essentials of Evangelical Theology*. 2 vols. New York: Harper & Rose, 1978.

Brooke, Penny Simpson. "Bowing to Family Pressure," Legal Questions. *Nursing 2005* 35, no. 4 (April 2005): 24. http://www.nursing2004.com.

Brooks, H. A. "Advantages and Value of Education." *Gospel Trumpet*, June 20, 1912, 4–5.

Brown, Charles E. "Women as Preachers." *Gospel Trumpet*, May 27, 1939, 5.

Byrum, E. E. "Should We Go to War?" *Gospel Trumpet*, April 14, 1898, 4.

Byrum, Russell R. *Christian Theology*. Anderson, IN: Gospel Trumpet Company, 1925.

———. "How Did God Inspire the Bible?" *Gospel Trumpet*, October 13, 1921, 4–5.

Callen, Barry L. *Faithful in the Meantime: A Biblical View of Final Things and Present Responsibilities.* Nappanee, IN: Evangel Publishing House, 1997.

——. *Preparing for Service: A History of Higher Education in the Church of God.* Anderson, IN: Warner Press, 1988.

——. *What We Teach.* Anderson, IN: Anderson University Press, 2005.

Callen, Barry L., ed. *Following the Light: Teachings, Testimonies, Trials and Triumphs of the Church of God Movement, Anderson.* Anderson, IN: Warner Press, 2000.

Campo-Flores, Arian. "The Legacy of Terri Schiavo." *Newsweek*, April 4, 2005, 22–28.

Carter, Jimmy. *Our Endangered Values: America's Moral Crisis.* New York: Simon & Schuster, 2005.

"Chicago Statement on Biblical Inerrancy." *Journal of the Evangelical Theological Society*, December 21, 1978, 289–296.

Church of God Ministries. *2005 Yearbook of the Church of God.* Anderson, IN: Church of God Ministries, 2005.

Clergy Task Force. *Go Preach My Gospel: Women in Ministry.* Second Editon. VHS. Anderson, IN: Church of God Ministries, 2004.

Collins, Sam. "Candles or Blowtorches?" *Church of God Peace Fellowship*, Winter 2004–5, 5. http://www.peacecog.com/newsletter/PF_Winter_04-05.pdf.

Cox, William E. *Amillennialism TODAY.* Philipsburg, NJ: Presbyterian and Reformed Publishing, 1966.

Dayton, Donald W. "The Battle for the Bible." *Christian Century*, November 10, 1976, 976–80.

DeVito, Joseph A. *Messages: Building Interpersonal Communication Skills,* 6th ed. New York: Pearson Education, 2005.

Dockery, David S., ed. *The Challenge of Postmodernism*. Grand Rapids, MI: Baker, 1995.

Eskridge, Larry. "Defining Evangelicalism." Wheaton, IL: Institute for the Study of American Evangelicals, Wheaton College, 1995. http://www.wheaton.edu/isae/defining_evangelicalism.html (accessed November 30, 2005).

Fee, Gordon, and Douglas Stuart. *How to Read the Bible for All It's Worth*. Grand Rapids, MI: Zondervan, 1993.

Flynn, Jeannette, et al. *Credentials Manual of the Church of God*. Revised Ed. Anderson, IN: Church of God Ministries, 2004.

Focus on the Family. "FOF Offers Insight into Terri Schiavo's Condition." News release, October 22, 2003. http://www.family.org/welcome/press/a0028513.cfm (accessed on December 7, 2005).

Foster, Richard J. *Streams of Living Water*. San Francisco: HarperSanFrancisco, 1998.

Gaulke, Max. *May Thy Kingdom Come—Now*. Anderson, IN: Warner Press, 1959.

Grady, J. Lee. *10 Lies the Church Tells Women: How the Bible Has Been Misused to Keep Women in Spiritual Bondage*. Lake Mary, Fla.: Creation House, 2000.

Gray, Albert F. *Christian Theology*. 2 vols. Anderson, IN: Gospel Trumpet Company, 1944.

Grenz, Stanley J. *Revisioning Evangelical Theology: A Fresh Agenda for the 21st Century*. Downers Grove, IL: InterVarsity Press, 1993.

Hazen, Robert J. "My Dual Citizenship." *Church of God Peace Fellowship*, Autumn 2004, 5. http://www.peacecog.com/newsletter/PF_Autmn_04.pdf.

Henry, William J. "Let the Fire Fall on Me." In *Worship the Lord: Hymnal of the Church of God*, 483. Anderson, IN: Warner Press, 1989.

Huber, Randal. *Called, Equipped and No Place to Go: Women Pastors and the Church.* Anderson, IN: Warner Press, 2003.

——. "Women Leaders in the Early Church." In Huber and Stanley, *Reclaiming the Wesleyan/Holiness Heritage.*

Huber, Randy, and John E. Stanley. *Reclaiming the Wesleyan/Holiness Heritage of Women Clergy: Sermons, a Case Study and Resources.* Grantham, PA: Wesleyan/Holiness Women Clergy, 1999. http://www.messiah.edu/whwc/booklets/reclaiming.html.

Johnson, A. Wayne. "Serving God in the Military Service." *Gospel Trumpet,* February 14, 1960, 9–10.

Koglin, Anna E. "The Status of Women in the Church." *Vital Christianity,* May 1, 1977, 17–18.

Leo, John. "End of the Affair." *U.S. News & World Report,* April 11, 2005. http://www.usnews.com/usnews/opinion/articles/050411/11john.htm.

Leonard, Juanita Evans. "Women, Change, and the Church." In Leonard, *Called to Minister,* 149–167.

Leonard, Juanita Evans, ed. *Called to Minister Empowered to Serve.* Anderson, IN: Warner Press, 1989.

Lindsell, Harold. *The Battle for the Bible.* Grand Rapids: Zondervan, 1976.

McNeal, Reggie. *Revolution in Leadership: Training Apostles for Tomorrow's Church.* Nashville: Abingdon, 1998.

Morrison, Laura J., et al. "Next-of-Kin Responses and Do-Not-Resuscitate Implications for Implantable Cardioverter Defibrillators," Letters. *Annals of Internal Medicine* 142, no. 8 (April 19, 2005): 676–77., http://www.annals.org/content/vol142/issue8/.

National Association of Evangelicals. "History of the NAE." http://www.nae.net/index.cfm?FUSEACTION=nae.history (accessed November 15, 2005).

Naylor, Charles W. "The Church's Jubilee." In *Worship The Lord: Hymnal of the Church of God*, 312. Anderson, IN: Warner Press, 1989.

——— . "Questions Answered." *Gospel Trumpet*, 38, no. 17 (April 25, 1918): 261–62.

——— . "The Reformation Glory," In *Worship the Lord: Hymnal of the Church of God*, 311. Anderson, IN: Warner Press, 1989.

Newell, Arlo E. "For Men Only? Breaking a Two Thousand Year-Old Tradition." *Vital Christianity*, May 1989, 12–13.

Newman, Troy. "The Blood of Martyrs Is the Seed of Christians." Voice for Terri Project, Operation Rescue, April 7, 2005. http://www.operationrescue.org/schiavo/ (accessed on December 7, 2005).

Oden, Thomas C. *Pastoral Theology: Essentials of Ministry.* San Francisco: HarperSanFranscisco, 1983.

Oldham, W. Dale. "Let Me See Jesus Only." In *Worship the Lord: Hymnal of the Church of God*, 451. Anderson, IN: Warner Press, 1989.

Packer, J. I. "Light in a Dark Place." In *Can We Trust the Bible?*, edited by Earl D. Radmacher, PPPP. Wheaton, IL: Tyndale House, 1979.

Pearson, Sharon. "Biblical Precedents of Women in Ministry." In Leonard, *Called to Minister*, 13–33.

Peterson, Eugene H. *Reversed Thunder.* San Francisco: HarperSanFrancisco, 1988.

Riggle, Herbert M. *Christ's Kingdom and Reign.* Anderson, IN: Gospel Trumpet Company, 1918.

Rogers, Jack, ed. Biblical *Authority.* Waco, TX: Word, 1977.

Rogers, Jack B., and Donald K. McKim. *The Authority and Inspiration of the Bible.* New York: Harper & Row, 1979.

Schell, William G. *A Better Testament: or Two Testaments Compared.* Moundsville, WV: Gospel Trumpet Publishing Co., 1899.

Smith, Frederick G. *Revelation Explained*. Anderson, IN: Gospel Trumpet Company, 1908.

———. *What the Bible Teaches*. Anderson, IN: Gospel Trumpet Co., 1914. 177.

Smith, F. G., E. E. Byrum, and J. W. Phelps, comps. "Teaching of the Church of God Concerning the Relationship of the Church to Civil Government and the Sacredness of Human Life and Our Attitude toward War." Anderson, IN: Executive Committee of the Missionary Board of the Church of God, 1917. Reprinted in *Church of God Peace Fellowship*, Spring 2005, 1–3. http://www.peacecog.com/newsletter/PF_Spring_05.pdf.

Smith, John W. V. *I Will Build My Church: Biblical Insights on Distinguishing Doctrines of the Church of God*. Anderson, IN: Warner Press, 1985.

———. *The Quest for Holiness and Unity*. Anderosn, IN: Warner Press, 1980.

Soc.Religion.Christianity. "Where Did All Those Denominations Come From?" From the FAQ collection of the Soc.Religion. Christianity Usenet newsgroup. http://geneva.rutgers.edu/src/faq/denominations-history.html (accessed November 30, 2005).

Stafford, Gilbert W. "Eschatology." Paper, Doctrinal Dialogue, North American Conference of the Church of God, Anderson, IN, June 30, 2004. http://www.anderson.edu/ccl/eschatology.pdf.

———. *Theology for Disciples*. Anderson, IN: Warner Press, 1996.

Stanley, John E. "New Testament Arguments for the Equality of Men and Women in Ministry." In Huber and Stanley, *Reclaiming the Wesleyan/Holiness Heritage*, PPPP.

Stanley, Susie. "Women Evangelists in the Church of God at the Beginning of the Twentieth Century." In Leonard, *Called to Minister*, 35–55.

Strege, Merle D. "The Demise (?) of a Peace Church: The Church of God (Anderson), Pacifism, and Civil Religion," *Mennonite Quarterly Report*, April, 1991, 128.

———. *I Saw the Church: The Life of the Church of God Told Theologically.* Anderson, IN: Warner Press, 2002.

———. "An Uncertain Voice for Peace." In *Proclaim Peace*, edited by Theron F. Schlabach and Richard T. Hughes, 115–127. Urbana, IL: University of Chicago Press, 1997.

Strong, Marie. *A Common Sense Approach to the Book of Revelation.* Edited by Sharon Clark Pearson. Anderson, IN: Warner Press, 1996.

Teasley, D. Otis. "Back to the Blessed Old Bible." In *Worship the Lord: Hymnal of the Church of God*, 354. Anderson, IN: Warner Press, 1989.

———. "Church of the Living God." In *Worship the Lord: Hymnal of the Church of God*, 281. Anderson, IN: Warner Press, 1989.

———. "We'll Crown Him Lord of All." In *Worship the Lord: Hymnal of the Church of God*, 217. Anderson, IN: Warner Press, 1989.

———. "We'll Praise the Lord." In *Worship the Lord: Hymnal of the Church of God*, 82. Anderson, IN: Warner Press, 1989.

Wallis, Jim. *God's Politics: Why the Right Gets It Wrong, and the Left Doesn't Get It.* San Francisco: HarperSanFrancisco, 2005.

Warner, Daniel S. "Fill Me with Thy Spirit, Lord." In *Worship the Lord: Hymnal of the Church of God*, 269. Anderson, IN: Warner Press, 1989.

———. "I Ought to Love My Savior." In *Worship the Lord: Hymnal of the Church of God*, 461. Anderson, IN: Warner Press, 1989.

Warner, D. S., and H. M. Riggle. *Cleansing the Sanctuary.* Moundsville, WV: Gospel Trumpet Co., 1903.

Webber, Robert. *The Younger Evangelicals.* Grand Rapids, MI: Baker Books, 2002.

Whitcomb, John C., Jr., and Henry M. Morris. *The Genesis Flood: The Biblical Record and Its Scientific Implications.* Philadelphia: The Presbyterian and Reformed Publishing Company, 1961.

Wickersham, H.C. *Holiness Bible Subjects,* 2nd ed. Grand Junction, MI: Gospel Trumpet Co., 1894.

Withrow, Oral, and Laura Withrow. *Meet Us at the Cross: An Introduction to the Church of God.* Anderson, IN: Warner Press, 1999.